Mary Astor's Purple Diary

ALSO BY EDWARD SOREL

WRITTEN AND ILLUSTRATED

Moon Missing
Making the World Safe for Hypocrisy
Superpen
The Zillionaire's Daughter
Johnny on the Spot
The Saturday Kid
Unauthorized Portraits
Literary Lives

ILLUSTRATED

Gwendolyn the Miracle Hen
King Carlo of Capri
Pablo Paints a Picture
The Pirates of Penzance
Word People
First Encounters
The Complete Fables of La Fontaine
The Mural at the Waverly Inn

MARY ASTOR'S PURPLE DIARY

THE GREAT AMERICAN SEX SCANDAL OF 1936

EDWARD SOREL

LIVERIGHT PUBLISHING COMPANY

A Division of W. W. Norton & Company

Independent Publishers Since 1923

New York • London

For information about permission to reproduce selections from this book,
write to Permissions, Liveright Publishing Corporation, a division of
W. W. Norton & Company, Inc., 500 Fifth Avenue, New York, NY 10110

For information about special discounts for bulk purchases, please contact
W. W. Norton Special Sales at specialsales@wwnorton.com or 800-233-4830

Manufacturing by Toppan Leefung Printing Limited

Library of Congress Cataloging-in-Publication Data

Names: Sorel, Edward, 1929– author.
Title: Mary Astor's Purple diary : the great American sex scandal of 1936 /
Edward Sorel.
Other titles: Purple diary
Description: First edition. | New York : Liveright Publishing Company,
a division of W. W. Norton & Company, [2016]
Identifiers: LCCN 2016012782 | ISBN 9781631490231 (hardcover)
Subjects: LCSH: Astor, Mary, 1906–1987—Comic books, strips, etc. | Motion
picture actors and actresses—United States—Biography—Comic books,
strips, etc. | Graphic novels.
Classification: LCC PN2287.A8 S67 2016 | DDC 791.4302/8092 [B] —dc23 LC
record available at https://lccn.loc.gov/2016012782

Liveright Publishing Corporation
500 Fifth Avenue, New York, N.Y. 10110
www.wwnorton.com

W. W. Norton & Company Ltd.
Castle House, 75/76 Wells Street, London W1T 3QT

1 2 3 4 5 6 7 8 9 0

For Madeline, Leo, Jenny, and Katherine

Mary Astor's Purple Diary

The Start of My Long Affair
with Mary Astor

I GUESS YOU COULD SAY Mary Astor and I "met cute," the
way romantic leads always do. It happened in 1965. I was
thirty-six, a freelance illustrator who, thanks to Vietnam, had
begun doing political satire in a left-wing magazine called *Ramparts*. I had long hair and dressed like a slob to show I wasn't one of
the "suits" who had gotten us into the war. Mary, as I would come
to call her, had retired from the screen a year earlier, after a career
often playing soigné, exquisitely coiffed upper-class women. She
was fifty-nine.

I had just married for the second time, and Nancy and I were lucky enough to find a railroad flat in one of the remaining tenements on Manhattan's Upper East Side. It was listed as a "professional apartment," meaning the renter had to run a business from home. In a rent-controlled building that meant the landlord could charge more. Still, I was delighted to pay the legal limit of $97.14 a month.

The place was a wreck, and Nancy insisted that the first thing we had to do was tear up the rotting linoleum in the kitchen. One layer yielded to another, until finally I came to a bunch of newspapers that had been laid over the warped wooden floor to make it level. They were issues of the New York *Daily News* and *Daily Mirror* from 1936.

The papers, nearly thirty years old, were smelly and yellow with

age, but otherwise readable. The giant black headlines concerned a child custody trial in Los Angeles. The *News* banner for August 1 screamed ASTOR'S BABY TO BE JUDGE. Next came ASTOR'S SENSATIONS SCARE FILM MOGULS. And by August 8 it was ASTOR DIARY "ECSTACY" (*sic*), with the subhead *G. S. KAUFMAN TRYST BARED*. I began piecing the pages together chronologically.

The Astor in question, I understood, was Mary. In 1936 she was only a featured player in movies, but enough of a star to make headlines when it came out that George S. Kaufman, then the most successful playwright on Broadway and married, had been her lover. Once his name emerged in Mary's child custody battle, the story pushed Hitler and Franco off tabloid front pages. I myself forgot the new linoleum and kept reading.

The scandal revolved around Mary's diary, which her ex-husband had found when they were still married. Its incriminating contents had forced Mary to give up custody of their daughter to her husband in order to obtain a divorce. But by 1936 she had decided to challenge the custody arrangement concerning their little girl. The husband planned to use the diary to prove she was an unfit mother. Mary, he claimed, had not only kept a tally of all her extramarital affairs but graded them. He threatened to put the document into evidence, and had already shown a page of it to the press. Although Mary had in fact used brown ink in her fountain pen, the tabloids couldn't resist making it jibe with the prose so they could call it "the Purple Diary."

My small collection of papers ran out before I learned the outcome of the trial, or whether Kaufman, then in Hollywood, had been forced to testify. *I had to know.* But further research would have to wait until I put down the new linoleum and met my deadlines.

One was for *Ramparts*, which was published in San Francisco. I had a monthly feature in it called "Sorel's Bestiary." Each month I caricatured liberal wafflers on Vietnam or right-wing war hawks as the birds they most resembled, and then wrote about their characteristics in the manner of an ornithologist. It was a visual device that was already old in the nineteenth century, but *Ramparts'* readers were hungry for any and all protest against the Vietnam War. When friends said how much they enjoyed one of my caricatures, I learned not to point out all the things that were wrong with the drawings. Nancy tried to teach me to simply say "thank you," but it's not easy when you yourself think your drawings are lousy. And they were. It took years before I began doing drawings I could take pride in.

My new agent kept bringing in assignments from ad agencies, which went a long way toward paying off the debts incurred from my first marriage. Whenever there was time between deadlines, I tried finding out all I could about Mary Astor. My curiosity was obviously prurient in nature, whetted by those 1936 tabloids. They had given me an itch to find out all I could about the scandal. (The word "prurient," if you care, first appeared in the sixteenth century, derived from the Latin verb *prurire*, "to itch.") Fortunately Mary had written a memoir in 1959, making it easy for me to scratch the surface of her life. I found a dog-eared copy at the Strand Book Store downtown, read it, and was hooked. She was smart, witty, and self-denigrating.

After reading her story I began to feel a real affection for her. And I thought she looked exactly like those beautiful women drawn by Charles Dana Gibson in the early 1900s. She was a "Gibson Girl" come to life.

But before I gave my heart to this stunning actress, I needed to know *everything* about her. If a new biography of Kaufman came out, I read it. If the Museum of Modern Art was showing a Mary Astor film, I saw it. And many years later, when the Internet made it possible, I was in touch with her daughter, Marylyn, who was living in a mobile home in Utah with a companion. She was the grandmother of eighteen children and the great-grandmother of twenty-two. In what she said online, Marylyn had nothing but kind words to say about *both* parents, upsetting my conviction, after reading Mary's memoir, that Daddy was the bad guy.

For half a century I promised myself that someday I would do a book about the Astor trial, but deadlines always got in the way. Then magazines stopped having much use for illustration. I have plenty of time now, but I'm old. When I started writing this book, I was already older than most people featured on the *Times* obituary page. So if some of these drawings look a little driven, you'll know why.

I soon became far more interested in Mary's entire life than in the scandal alone. I began thinking about illustrating her biography. That would give me a chance to draw New York as it was in the 1920s and 1930s, and Hollywood when glamorous women sashayed down the street in flowing dresses and wide-brimmed hats.

That scene is a far cry from the Bronx where I was born and grew up. As a latchkey kid who could do whatever he wanted after school,

I would draw pictures and go to the movies. Mom was a sewing machine operator and union organizer in a millinery factory; she was proud of my drawings. My father, a door-to-door peddler of dry goods in suburban Long Island before there were shopping centers, was not. He knew artists starved, and also worried that I didn't play stickball in the street like the other boys. He thought I should go to a military school so I could become a man, even though he himself had fled Poland in 1918 to escape military service.

Around the corner from us was the seedy art deco Luxor movie house, where films from Warner Brothers and 20th Century played after they had played everywhere else. But even the rundown Luxor

SATURDAY MATINEES INCLUDED A NEWSREEL, A BUGS BUNNY, A CHAPTER OF DICK TRACY, TWO MOVIES, AND AT LEAST ONE LAUREL AND HARDY SHORT. THAT'S ME COVERING MY EYES SO I WON'T SEE WHAT HAPPENS TO OLLIE NEXT. IF I WATCH I'LL   LAUGH SO HARD THAT I'LL WET MY PANTS.

drew a translucent curtain over the screen when the film ended, just as the big movie palaces in Manhattan did. Four blocks down was the more impressive Loew's 167th Street, which showed MGM and Paramount films. The interior couldn't compare to Loew's Paradise farther uptown, which had a ceiling of twinkling stars, moving clouds, and flying birds, but it did have sculptured figurines on the walls. All theaters in the Bronx offered double features, and I often took in four movies on a weekend. I knew the names of all the actors, even those with bit roles—Donald Meek, Leonid Kinsky, Zasu Pitts, Eric Blore, Louise Beaver, Franklin Pangborn, and the like. . . . It was these ubiquitous supporting actors whom I saw week after week who would become part of my family—the part that wasn't always arguing about whether Stalin or Trotsky was the savior of the working class.

Mary Astor, however, was not an important member of my movie family. The first time I saw her was in *The Prisoner of Zenda* when I was ten, and I do remember puzzling over why someone so incredibly beautiful was desperate to marry Raymond Massey, who was scheming and homely. The husbands Mary chose in real life seemed equally unfathomable, along with so many of her decisions—until you know about her tyrannical Kraut of a father, Otto Ludwig Wilhelm Langhanke.

Whatever I know about this Teutonic fathead I learned from Mary's memoir, *My Story*. It's true that her dedication reads, "For my mother and father with love because I understand them now," but when she wrote that book she was under the influence of a sympathetic priest in the Roman Catholic Church, and she was angling for the sacrament of reconciliation. Yet what she actually *says* about

Mommy and Daddy leaves no doubt they were the parents from hell, which for Mary was located right there in their clapboard house on the outskirts of Quincy, Illinois. If hell is a place without any joy, the Langhanke home qualified.

Otto, who had come from Berlin in 1889 when he was eighteen, carried with him the Old World belief that all children are obliged to provide for their parents. Having a nasty martinet for a father wouldn't have been so damaging to Mary if she'd had a nurturing mother, or if they had allowed her to have friends and visit their houses. But Mary, who was born in Quincy, was never allowed to have close friendships with others her own age, or see how other parents treated their children. And Helen seemed clearly as frightened of Otto as her daughter was, and both mother and child constantly deferred to his various harebrained schemes. When Otto, who had come to America for the express purpose of getting rich, proved to be as ham-handed raising chickens as he was at everything else, he was forced to take a job teaching German at the local high school in Quincy. Helen and Mary (born Lucile) would tend to the hens.

In 1917 President Woodrow Wilson had Congress declare war on Germany so that the "world would be safe for democracy." Once the country was at war, the language of the Huns was cut from the Illinois school curriculum, and Otto, who had not only taught German but also written a book teaching German grammar, was fired. There was no farewell party. After months of listening to Otto's impassioned defense of the Kaiser Wilhelm, who would have attended?

My guess is that around this time Herr Langhanke began eying his luscious eleven-year-old daughter as a possible way out of poverty. He had read about huge salaries being paid to young women in New York—girls, really—for acting in the movies. Not one of them was as pretty as his Lucile. Otto knew she pored over magazines like *Motion Picture* and *Shadowland*. Perhaps she, too, dreamed she could be an actress. So one night when Lucile showed no interest in practicing the piano or cracking the books he had commanded she read, he asked his child, "Don't you want to be somebody?"

> Daddy, I am somebody [a quaint notion she was soon to
>   forfeit]. I am myself.
> Well, what do you want to do then?
> I just want to grow up, and go to high school and maybe
>   Gem City Business College. I want to work a little, and
>   then get married and have children.

Otto erupted. Lucile was a lazy good-for-nothing; she had "no ambition." He pushed her on to the piano bench and pounded the top of the upright to emphasize his fury. Lucile was too shaken by his violence to hear everything he was saying, but she remembered phrases like *hoi polloi* and *after all we are sacrificing for you*. Helen stood in the doorway crying and pleading, "Daddy, don't hurt her, don't hurt her!" He turned and shouted, *"YOU KEEP OUT OF THIS!!!"*

That wasn't the last tirade that Lucile would endure about the need to make something of herself, and it didn't take her long to figure out what that something was. Two years after the war ended, in June of 1920, when Lucile was fourteen, Otto sold the farm and all their possessions and put his family on the train to New York. By Jove, she was to be *a movie star!*

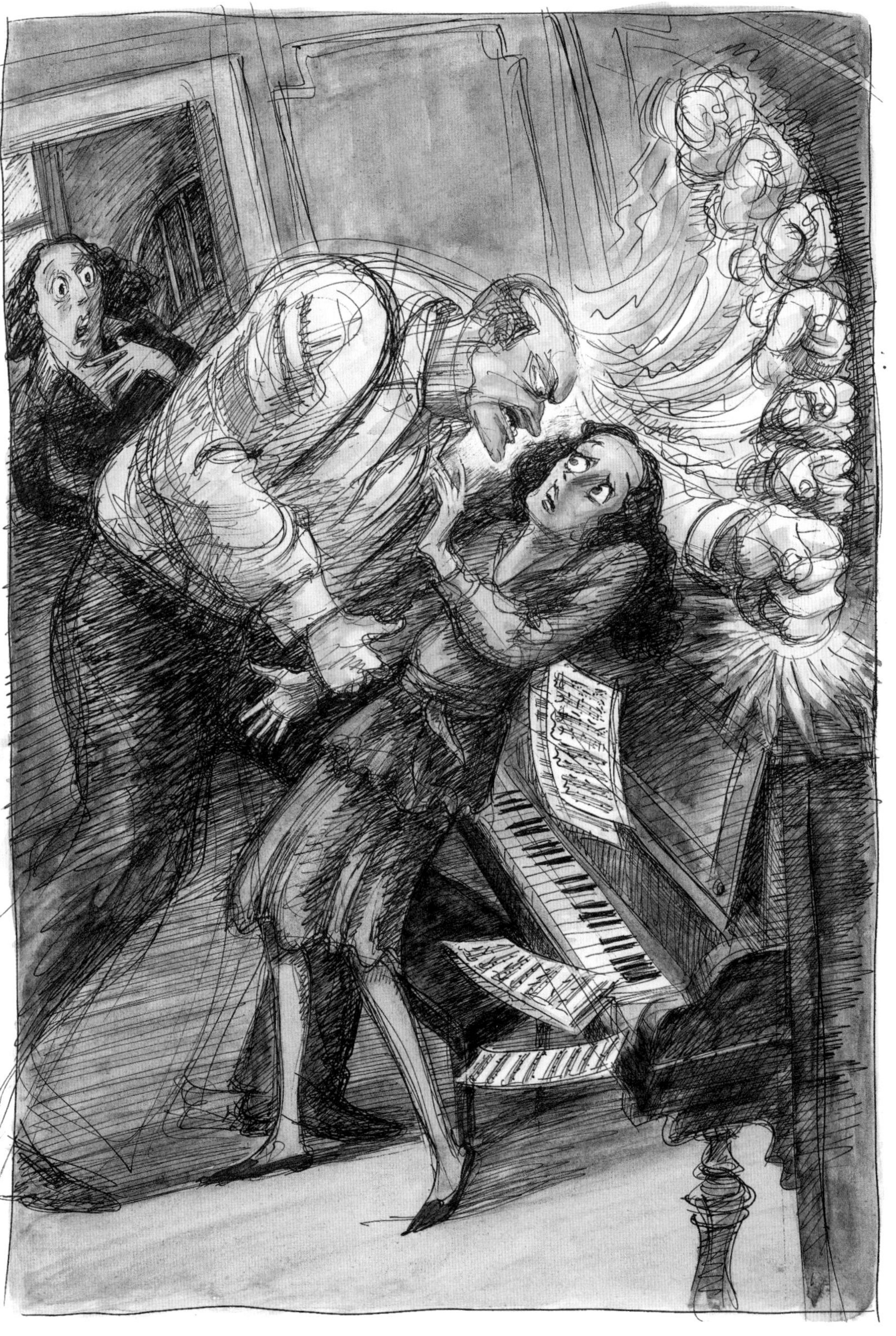

As usual, Otto blundered. Unaware that most movie production was shifting to the West Coast, he confidently arrived in New York with a list of every studio in the Bronx, Brooklyn, New Jersey, and towns on Long Island. Since over eight hundred feature films were released every year—as opposed to the fewer than five hundred today—filming was still taking place on the East Coast, and Otto managed to arrange auditions for his daughter at a few of the lesser companies.

At the Eugene Brewster Studios, Charles Albin, one of the foremost photographers in New York, spotted Lucile and asked Otto whether he could take her picture. Once Daddy was assured there would be no charge, he eagerly agreed. Albin was a painter with natural light and did no retouching. In the high-minded bohemia of his photographic studio, she also had her first exposure to a dedicated artist working for more than the almighty dollar.

Albin had originally aspired to take holy orders, perhaps the reason he was able to pull off an extraordinary early portrait of his subject as a "Madonna-child," his name for Lucile's look. So captivated was he by her cascade of luxuriant auburn hair, her deep blue eyes, and what he regarded as her virginal beauty that he arranged an audition for her with his friend D. W. Griffith, the most innovative and respected film director in America.

When Lucile arrived at the Griffith studio in Mamaroneck, in New York's Westchester County, she was met by none other than her idol, Lillian Gish, the star of many of Griffith's films. Miss Gish, as kind and caring in life as she was on the screen, helped with makeup and whispered tips about what to do. She had just completed directing her younger sister, Dorothy, in the feature film

Remodeling Her Husband, and knew exactly what was required. The screen test went well. Realizing this, Otto began badgering the director about what salary he might expect. Griffith sized him up as a "walking cash register" and showed them the door.

This would hardly be the last time the parasitic papa would foul up his daughter's career. Otto had absolutely no sense of his effect on people and always assumed he was the cagiest cat in the room. By God, if an educated German couldn't get rich in this country of vulgar bunny hug dancers and uninhibited black jazzmen, it was only because he wasn't trying hard enough.

But hard as Otto did try, by September Lucile still had no contract. He and Helen began worrying about rent money and food. Otto tried selling some movie plots based on German stories he had translated, including *Elga* by the kaiser's favorite dramatist, Hermann Sudermann. He brought them to Harry Durant, head of the writing department at Famous Players–Lasky. Durant wasn't interested, but his eyebrows rose when Otto idly showed him the folder of Albin shots, which he always carried with him just in case. Durant told Otto to bundle his would-be breadwinner off to the Famous Players offices in midtown Manhattan for an audition.

The thin little family was one step away from the abyss when they suddenly found themselves in the presence of Jesse L. Lasky himself. Lucile was clumsily clad in a taffeta dress and brown Oxfords. But she did as she was told—"*Stand up and walk over there. . . . Now turn around . . .*"—and suddenly everyone was talking at once. The miracle had happened: she had a six-month contract at—hold on to your hats—*sixty dollars a week!* And days later she had a ritzy new name, supplied by Lasky in consultation with the publicity department. Lucile Vasconcellos Langhanke was now . . .

MARY ASTOR

I can only guess one reason why they chose a name that smacked of high society. It was the way Mary spoke. Ever since she was a child, Otto had badgered his daughter to enunciate clearly, and she succeeded so well that her classmates said she talked funny. To Lasky her perfect elocution must have suggested elegance, and what could be more elegant than an allusion to *the* Mrs. Astor and her four hundred pedigreed peers?

Lasky assured Mr. and Mrs. Langhanke that the studio planned to develop Mary into a star, and suggested they help by taking her to some Broadway plays. The fourteen-year-old had never been to the theater. Of course, Otto wouldn't take her to the *Ziegfeld Follies* or Earl Carroll's *Scandals of 1920*, but *The Girl from Utah*, a London import, sounded suitable. Because English audiences arrived at a theater before intermission, British producers saved their best material for the second act. So when *The Girl from Utah* was imported to Broadway, where the public came for the overture, Jerome Kern was hired to write new songs for the first act. One of them was the memorable "They Didn't Believe Me," a song with the easy cadence of everyday speech that changed forever the way popular ballads would be written. As it turned out, Mary loved the show, while Herr Langhanke preferred *The Merry Countess*, starring the Dolly Sisters, since it was based on *Die Fledermaus* and had music by Johann Strauss.

On another day Mary and her mother toured the Famous

Players–Lasky Studios in Astoria, Long Island, gaping at Rudolph Valentino and Bebe Daniels emoting on one stage and Ethel Clayton on another. Mae Murray, the current rage, sparkled by, dressed in diamonds and satin.

After several weeks of bit parts, Mary got the lead in a two-reeler silent called *The Beggar Maid* and had the thrill of seeing her name up in lights when it opened on Broadway at the palatial, marble-columned Rivoli. The homeschooling that Otto insisted on was abandoned so she could take voice lessons twice a week, and dancing lessons three times a week with the modern-dance pioneers Ruth St. Denis and Ted Shawn at their Denishawn School. Mary, everyone soon learned, didn't have much of a singing voice, but she loved dancing.

By the time she was sixteen she had been a featured player in half a dozen films, and was signed to a new one-year contract with Famous Players for five hundred dollars a week. Otto quite naturally began wearing custom-made suits, even twirling a malacca cane.

No sooner had Daddy bought an apartment in Jackson Heights, Queens, however, than Famous Players announced it was sending Mary to the West Coast for a film. Otto decided Helen should guard their golden teen in Hollywood while he blew her earnings by having work done on the new place. Mary knew she had better act shattered at being separated from him, but her heart raced with joy at the thought of being in dazzling Hollywood without Daddy's nagging criticism and scowling presence.

Mary Meets America's Greatest
Shakespearean Actor

M ARY WAS DELIRIOUS to have landed in Hollywood, and I, as her self-appointed Boswell, felt better myself. Now I'd be able to draw that exotic place when it was just at the beginning of its love affair with art deco,

IN 1923 TOM MIX, STAR OF WESTERNS, ADDED THIS TWO-DOOR LEACH TO HIS LARGE COLLECTION OF LUXURY CARS. THE LEACH, MANUFACTURED IN LOS ANGELES ESCHEWED RUNNING BOARDS IN FAVOR OF METAL FOOTSTANDS.

and when automobiles were becoming the favorite status symbol for the stars.

Thanks to her having kept a diary even as a teenager, Mary was able to give the exact date of her arrival in Hollywood: April 19, 1923, two weeks before her seventeenth birthday. She and her mother checked into the Hollywood Hotel on Hollywood Boulevard, a wide three-story stucco structure in the Spanish Mission style, surrounded by swaying palm trees. It was described by one of Mary's movie magazines as a "popular rendezvous for the younger set." But there wasn't much chance of Mary's interacting with any of them. Helen would see to that.

From their windows facing the Hollywood Hills, they could see enormous, 45-foot-tall letters being erected on one of the mountains. Studded with four thousand light bulbs, they would soon spell out HOLLYWOODLAND, the name of a real estate development that advertised itself as a "superb environment without excessive cost on the Hollywood side of the hills."

That same year of 1923 also saw the opening of Tutankhamen's tomb in Egypt, the establishment of the Union of Soviet Socialist Republics in Russia, and the arrival of Walt and Roy Disney in Los Angeles, where Disney Brothers Studio would produce animated cartoons. In New York, Lee De Forest demonstrated his sound on films. The movie to see was *The Hunchback of Notre Dame* starring Lon Chaney.

Helen refused to take Mary to see it, fearing she was still too young to watch a horror movie. After a few days of touring their exciting new environment, they were summoned to the Famous Players studio, and Mary was cast in *The Marriage Maker*, starring Jack Holt. Arriving each morning and spotting Gloria Swanson,

Pola Negri, or Nita Naldi smoking a cigarette in a foot-long holder was glam, but having a director bark out her every movement and gesture through a megaphone as the camera rolled grew mechanical. When, she wondered, did acting become creative?

Mary was in the middle of her second assignment, *Woman Proof*, when word came of an offer so dazzling she couldn't fathom it. According to a top executive at her studio, Warner Brothers wanted to borrow her to play opposite John Barrymore—JOHN BARRYMORE!—in his next picture, *Beau Brummel*. Warner's was prepared to pay Famous Players–Lasky eleven hundred dollars for the privilege, though Mary would receive none of the money.

Wasting no time, Otto sprang onto a train headed for Los Angeles. Barging into the offices of any executives he could find, he demanded, threatened, and finally pleaded for a share of this windfall. It did no good. Otto could only seethe.

Acquiring Mary Astor as his leading lady was an impulse purchase by Barrymore. He had never met her or seen her onscreen; he'd only seen her Albin portrait in a movie magazine. It was the same one that had cinched her contract with Famous Players, but this time it carried the caption "On the Brink of Womanhood." Later, when Mary asked why he had chosen her, he confessed to his infatuation with the image. If her portrait had inflamed more earthly desires, he did not speak of them.

Because *Beau Brummel* would be Barrymore's first film for Warner's—his previous movie, *Sherlock Holmes*, was for Goldwyn— the brothers Warner were eager to grant their prestigious star his every wish. He was then at the peak of his celebrity, having just completed his revolutionary interpretation of *Hamlet* on Broadway. His

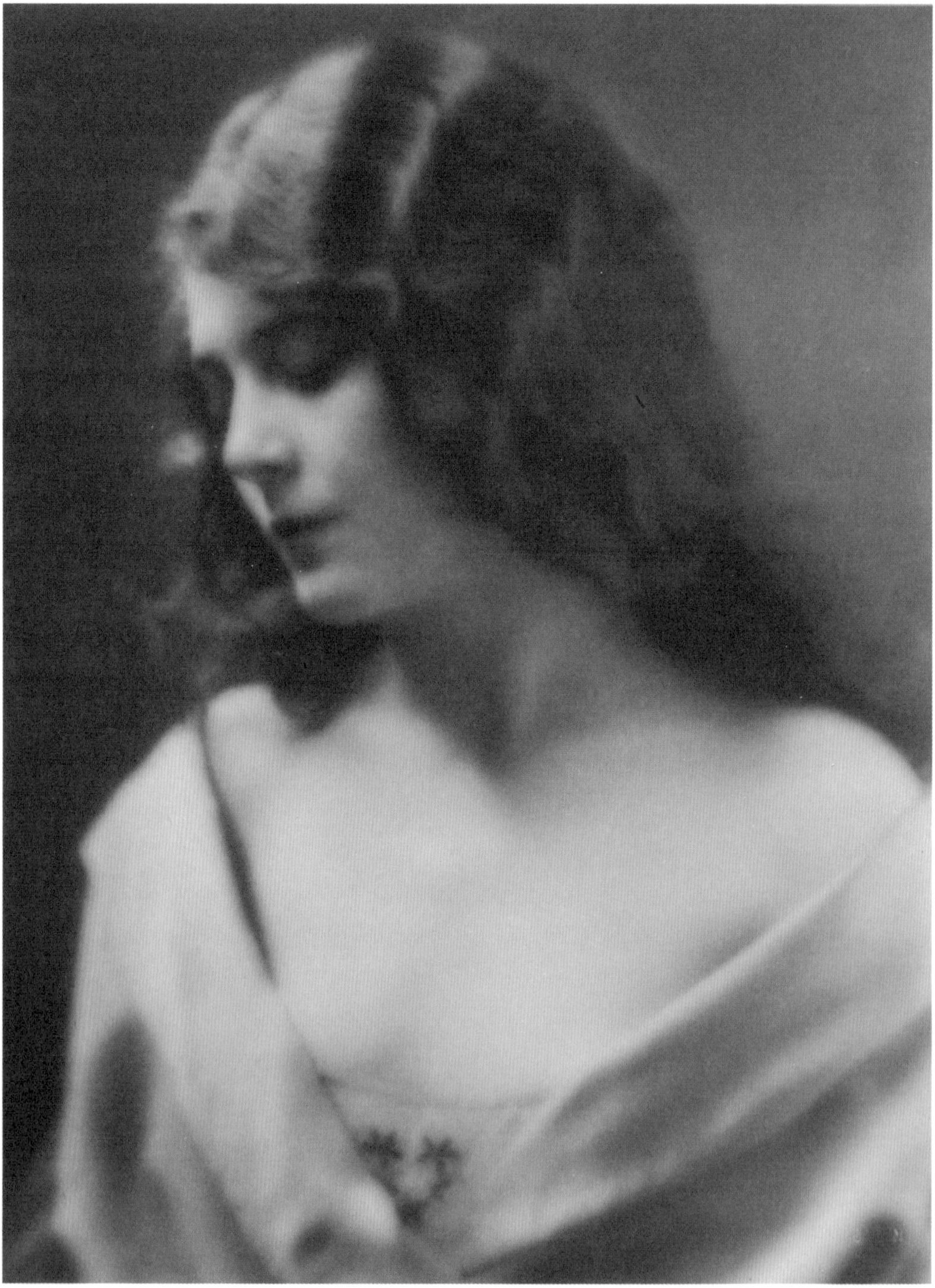

performance did away with the Victorian ideal of the "Sweet Prince" and replaced it with Freudian brooding. The critics hailed his Hamlet as one of the greatest ever seen in New York, and the production ran for 101 performances, one more than Edwin Booth's run in 1864–65, nearly sixty years earlier.

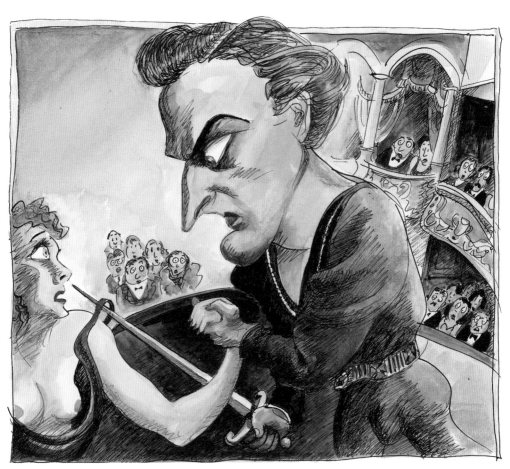

Barrymore had also bested his older brother, Lionel, whose *Macbeth* had closed a year earlier after a short run. John, like an emperor of ancient Rome, had every reason to believe he'd become a god, and could have anything he wanted, including that innocent beauty on the brink of womanhood whom he had seen in *Photoplay*.

How many virgins Barrymore deflowered in his lifetime remains unknowable, but we know that at eighteen the handsome devil seduced Evelyn Nesbit, a sixteen-year-old showgirl. In the course of their romance she was admitted to a hospital for an appendectomy, which many at the time believed was a code word for something less acceptable. Their romance might have survived that trauma had not her stage mother pushed her into the arms of the celebrated architect Stanford White, who became her ardent suitor. Later Evelyn married the high-society millionaire Harry Thaw—who then shot and killed White in a scandalous 1904 society murder that shocked the country. Thaw believed it was White who had stolen his wife's irreplaceable virginity, thereby making it, in Thaw's eyes, justifiable homicide. If the *real* culprit had taken the bullet, Mary's life would have played out very differently.

But to return to what happened to Mary Astor, we must go to the Warner studio where the first meeting between the teenage innocent and the forty-one-year-old roué took place. Lights and cameras were set up to see how they photographed together. Beau's eighteenth-century costume made "The Great Profile" seem even more killing in person than in his photographs. As the lights were adjusted, Mary knew her awkwardness showed. Barrymore turned on the charm, making her feel they were both professionals involved in a silly enterprise unworthy of their talents. When the time came for them to align their silhouettes, he whispered, "You are so goddamned beautiful you make me feel faint."

Mary, as she later revealed in her memoir, was instantly, madly,

and completely in love with him, and he apparently with her—since even the most expert seducer may occasionally transcend himself. But they understood from the start that their attachment would have to remain clandestine. Certainly her parents must never have an inkling of *anything*. And if the Warner brothers, much less the public, ever heard that their still-married headliner was romantically involved with his leading lady offscreen, it would be curtains for Mary's career playing virgins. There was also the little matter of California's statutory rape law, which could have put America's greatest Hamlet behind bars for up to four years.

The soon-to-be lovers had to be careful. Even during the intimate scenes, they never forgot that many eyes were upon them. Jack had the prop man place their two camp chairs next to each other off the set, but they were never out of Helen's field of vision. Getting Mary alone would require strategy. He began coming to the Langhanke apartment near the studio for dinner, praising Helen's gravity-lowering goulash and silently listening to Otto's racial theories. These boiled down to the unquestionable fact that the German race had produced the greatest geniuses in art, music, and literature. As a member of that race, Otto found it insufferable that he was now forced to deal with, as he saw it, his inferiors, a bunch of illiterate, lecherous Jews who cared only about money.

Barrymore held his tongue. He was prepared to endure anything as long as he eventually took Mary over the brink into womanhood. He even cut down on his expletives and curbed his drinking while with the Langhankes.

After a few meals the actor took Otto aside. "She doesn't know what it's all about, but I think she can learn." He offered to teach Mary the skills she lacked, and came often to work on her diction, while mother and father eavesdropped in the next room. "I feel she's too self-conscious," he finally told them. "She's too afraid of what you are thinking instead of listening to me." When they hesitated about allowing her to study with him at the Beverly Hills Hotel, he knew what they feared—"Don't be ridiculous! This is a kid."

A plan was set in motion. On Sundays his car would pick up Mary for her alleged acting lessons. There, in his suite filled with flowers, he waited for her to outgrow her inhibitions. Coming from a physically cold family, she was repelled by even a kiss. Having no other choice, the seducer bided his time and introduced her to tenderness and gaiety, neither of which she had ever experienced at home. He taught her how to finesse social occasions by regarding etiquette as no more than "considerate behavior." He showed her his collection of rare books and gave her many volumes on art, music, drama, and poetry. More important, he tried to give her a sense of her own worth. "Until you break away from their domination, they'll stifle you. They'll just make a meal ticket out of you. And you're the only one who can do anything about it."

I want to believe that when Mary finally did give in to him, she did so eagerly. Yet his carefully planned strategy to overcome her modesty and occupy her maidenhead seems less a romantic wooing than a calculated campaign designed to achieve victory at all cost. It smacks of trickery and an unconcern for what the consequences might be for his underage virgin. It was, we must assume, in his hotel room that Mary first imbibed a glass of alcohol. Mary in her memoir says they spoke of marriage plans. But neither told a soul about them. Both knew it was too preposterous a notion to confide to anyone.

With filming on *Brummel* over, Jack made ready to go to Philadelphia, Boston, and Washington to tour with *Hamlet*. He and Mary somehow managed a few minutes apart from the Langhankes to say their goodbyes. As they clung to each other, the actor begged her to be true to him. "You have become wise at deception. Don't use it against me. I need your fidelity; I need to know that there is someone in the world who can be faithful."

These recollections are also from Mary's memoir. She was so

utterly in love with him that almost every word he said appeared to have stayed with her for life. He was not only her first love, but also, she would have us believe, her great love. In *My Story*, written years later when she was fifty-three, she still believed he had intended to marry her.

Their separation lasted far longer than either had anticipated. Mary made some trips to New York for work, but by the time Barrymore got there, she was back in Hollywood; and then *Hamlet* went to London. Since her parents opened Mary's letters, Jack had to be circumspect. She too couldn't write how she really felt, since they read her outgoing mail as well, and even her diary, she suspected. She was not allowed out of the house alone—my god, there were mailboxes out there!—nor could she close her bedroom door. Otto and Helen were certain that whatever Mary would do in private was something she shouldn't be doing.

Here's a copy of the three-sheet poster that was printed when

Beau Brummel opened. How weird was it for Mary to pass that gigantic image of herself, knowing the woman in Beau Brummel's arms wasn't even allowed to walk down the street without her mother?

But Douglas Fairbanks Sr., America's top swashbuckler, didn't know Mary was a puppet operated by her parents. If she was good enough for Barrymore, she might be adequate as *his* leading lady in *Don Q, Son of Zorro.* He invited the teenager to lunch at Pickfair, the magnificent estate he shared with his blond, blue-eyed wife, Mary Pickford, dubbed "America's Sweetheart." Among the other guests was the British-born novelist Elinor Glyn, sixty-one, who knew everyone in Hollywood. At the dining table Glyn sat erect in her chair, as if to remind everyone that she was a member of the aristocracy on her mother's side. Being a descendant of Lord Duffus didn't alter her financial need to write lots of racy novels and screenplays to stay in the fast lane. The tabloid-reading public took seriously her pronouncements about who had "It" (as Clara Bow did) and who didn't.

Over things in aspic the subject of Mary's suitability for the role of Dolores de Muro, a young Spanish senorita, came up. Her freckles could be dealt with, but Miss Glyn declared that her curls were all wrong for the type. Rising royally from the table, she scooped up some butter from a bowl and began massaging it into Mary's hair. "*There!*"—she said, pulling it into a tight bun and jabbing in a decorative comb. "*That's* how the child should wear it!" Mary sat rigid and stone-faced, uncertain which was more degrading, having her head greased or being called a child.

She got the role, but there was more ignominy to come. Mary

soon realized that unlike Barrymore, the forty-two-year-old Fairbanks was embarrassed to do love scenes, and far less interested in
acting than in athletic movement. This time he was going to stag-
ger his public by his way with a bullwhip. How he trained! From
her dressing room Mary heard the endless *smack* of his growing
virtuosity. The trainer was supposed to handle the close-ups, like
snatching a cigarette from someone's mouth with the rawhide, but
in a stunt where he was to sneak up on a startled Dolores, Doug
insisted he could manage. Still smarting from Glyn's insult, Mary
refused a double, wanting to prove her maturity. Two takes went
beautifully—the twenty-foot whip nuzzled her shoulders like a sly
suitor. But the star wanted just one more, and this time he miscal-
culated, lashing her neck.

Doug, horrified at the pain he had caused, stuttered and stam-
mered his profound apologies. But when the actor-director Donald
Crisp suffered the same fate (this time the whip was wielded by
the professional), he gave out the order "From now on we stick to
dummies."

At long last Mary heard the news she had been longing for. After
seventeen months she would be leaving Los Angeles for New York,
exactly when Barrymore was due to dock there—May 5, 1925.

Six days before their meeting Barrymore was on the pier at
Southampton, about to board the SS *Olympic* for home, when a
reporter from the *New York Evening Post* asked him to comment
on his tour. The actor loftily offered his belief that "Shakespearean
drama probably would do more to bind the British and American peoples together than any other force." He admitted he was
returning to act in a movie, but after that, he promised, he would

certainly return to the stage, perhaps in *King Lear*. Although he had already marked up his copy with passages he planned to cut, he also feared how draining it would be to play that demanding role night after night. Hamlet was bad enough. In fact he would never play Lear.

As her first love was sailing toward New York, Mary was doing last-minute retakes on *Don Q* and posing for publicity shots. When she was finally about to board the train, she found that a crowd of friends and publicity people had come to see her off. Once in her drawing room, she found it bedecked with orchids from United Artists, the producers of *Don Q*. So this was what it was like to be a movie star.

Mary and her parents found their apartment in Jackson Heights also filled with flowers—those from Jack. As he emerged from his cab, Mary slipped downstairs and fell into his arms. Then he and "Goopher," his pet name for her, extinguished all signs of ardor before entering the Langhanke living room to begin catching up.

Jack told about his triumphant season in London and his long vacation fishing for salmon in Norway. He didn't volunteer that his drinking had made it mandatory for him to dry out in a sanatorium there, far from English or American reporters. Otto, in turn, boasted about the Moorish monstrosity he had bought on Temple Hill Drive in the Hollywood Hills, using the big bucks his daughter was now making from her new contract with First National. The home even came equipped with a maid, a gardener, a Pierce-Arrow limousine, and a chauffeur. And to boot Chaplin—yes, Chaplin— had once lived there.

The following day Mary met her lover in his suite at the Ambassador Hotel, and it seemed to her nothing had changed—neither their passion for each other nor their desire to marry. "It was just as I had dreamed of it during that lonely year and a half," she wrote thirty-four years later. Jack told her of his plans to do *Richard III* in London next season and have her play Lady Anne. "You will learn the part, and I will help you become the actress you should be."

When Barrymore was again chez Langhanke, he gingerly brought up the idea of Mary's acting alongside him. Otto dismissed it out of hand—the difference between studio and theater pay was too great. Jack waited in vain for a vital sign from Mary. The nineteen-year-old actress knew this was the chance of a lifetime. The class perks that meant so much to her father didn't matter to her. She made the money; why, *why* couldn't she assert herself? For

Barrymore, it was a reminder that she was still "on the brink of womanhood," but not yet a woman.

When Mary showed up at the hotel the next day, Jack was already drinking. "You haven't changed a bit," he said with bitter disappointment. *"Nothing has changed."*

But for him, everything had changed. Seducing a girl was one thing, but marrying one still subservient to the will of her father would be quite another. He was done with being followed everywhere by her appalling parents. When Mary's contract made it impossible for her to act with Barrymore in his next film, *The Sea Beast*, based on *Moby-Dick*, the actor cast Dolores Costello as Ahab's love interest. And before the film was over it was this new beauty he wanted for his third wife.

I'm sympathetic to Barrymore's dilemma, but he should have been up front with Mary about his new feelings. Yet he felt he couldn't be candid because he and Mary were under contract to costar in the forthcoming production of *Don Juan*. How could she, much less any woman, pretend to be in love with him if he told her it was over? He decided not to make a clean break, but Mary couldn't help feeling his remoteness on and off the set. She tried to win him back by saying that she had finally declared her independence from her father, that her mother would no longer be in constant attendance, and that she would now be allowed to go wherever she pleased. "Well, that's some progress," he said.

On what was thought to be the last day of shooting, Mary waited until they were away from the film crew. With her heart, as she recalled, rapidly beating in fear, she asked him once and for all if he truly felt nothing for her. She couldn't remember exactly how she phrased the question, but she always remembered his answer.

Don Juan (1926) is now remembered not for its offstage melo-drama but for its background-music soundtrack, the harbinger of the talkies, which came the following year and affected our heroine as well as so many other silent stars.

The Great Escape and the
Very Nice Starter Husband

I'VE SEEN A LOT of movies in the last eighty years, but the ones I try to avoid are those where an innocent woman falls hopelessly in love with a cad who breaks her heart. It's hard to sit through that one, so I won't spend any time describing the agonies Mary endured after the Great Man gave her the kiss-off. Her melancholy was hardly ameliorated by her father's endless lectures and faultfinding or her parents' eternal bickering. Mary's diary entry for May 5, 1926, reads, "We seem like a tinder ready to flame up at any moment."

I'd also like to skip the pall cast by Mary's father over her adolescence. It reminds me too much of my own. My father, Morris Schwartz, had little education, but he did share with Otto the expectation of financial support from his offspring—another reason my father took such a dim view of my drawing. How was I going to support *him* by drawing pictures? But I lucked out: my mother, the former Rebecca Kleinberg, wouldn't put up with his put-downs. She knew I had talent, and she even knew where I got it: from *her* father, Hyman Kleinberg, who had gone to tailoring school in Bucharest.

WHAT I REMEMBER ABOUT GRANDPA'S STORE WAS THE TINY ROOM IN THE BACK, CLOSED OFF BY A CURTAIN, WHERE MEN IN THE NEIGHBORHOOD PLAYED PINOCHLE. IT ALSO HID A BARREL OF RED WINE LONG AFTER PROHIBITION HAD ENDED.

Of course, from his shop in the Bronx he mainly sent out clothes to be cleaned and just did sewing and pressing, but he *could* design elegant clothes when asked. It was due to that genetic inheritance from Papa Kleinberg, Mom believed, that I was destined to be an artist. (When I ridiculed the idea, my daughter Katherine said, "Well, being a tailor, like being an artist, does require right-brain strength.")

This seems as good a time as any to explain how Eddie Schwartz morphed into Edward Sorel. You can see why on so many levels I had to rebel against my father, so after I landed my first good-paying job ($85 a week) at *Esquire* magazine, I decided to have my last name legally changed. I chose Sorel because I had read Stendahl's *The Red and the Black*, that nineteenth-century novel about an ambitious bounder who is catnip to women and rises socially beyond his provincial upbringing. Like me, Julien Sorel hated his father, the clergy, and the corrupt society of his time. Even the fact that he ended up guillotined appealed to me. Surely I'd end up the same, considering all the left-wing committees I was on during the McCarthy hysteria. Although plainly I wasn't beheaded, I did get a visit from an FBI agent in 1959 after I published a few issues of *Sorel's Affiche.*

The *Affiche* was a broadside in which I satirized anything that came into my head, usually of a political nature. For the first two issues I asked my friend Warren Miller to write the text. Warren, a well-known novelist, had once been a member of the Communist Party, like many of my older friends. That may explain what happened after the second issue of *Sorel's Affiche* was mailed to hundreds of art directors in New York.

I had hoped my illustrated promotion piece would bring some jobs my way. What it brought instead was a grim FBI agent at my door, claiming to be from an investment firm (which he refused to identify) that was considering investing in my "periodical." I quickly pegged him for what he was—which I'm certain he meant for me to do—but I answered all his questions about my "aims." After he left I smiled at the idea I was considered a potential threat to my country's security. I haven't felt that powerful since.

Now where were we? Oh yes, Barrymore dumped Mary. Well, if you thought Mary's mother would offer her solace, you don't know Helen Langhanke. She knew what had happened between the great actor and her daughter, but she not only continued to support Otto in his outrageous exploitation; she also seems never to have really liked her own child. When Otto denounced Mary over how lazy she had become, Helen could only nod piously. One night Mary actually fainted from the onslaught of abuse. Even after she had been put to bed, his voice could be heard outside the door—*"But you will try to do what Daddy has told you, won't you?"* Then he barged in for a final harangue.

Mary lay awake in bed for the next two hours until she was certain they were both asleep. She threw on some clothes, packed a few things, and went out on the balcony that reached a small cypress bent low enough for her to manage her escape. It was after two in the morning when she reached Hollywood Boulevard and checked into a small hotel. She stayed in bed late, smiling in the knowledge that on that day no one would command, dictate, or arrange her life. She had learned one of life's essential lessons: If you can't fight, flee.

A week later a neighbor sympathetic to Mary, now twenty-one, arranged a meeting between her and her now subdued father. Otto agreed to deposit a whole $500 in her personal checking account, and she was given her liberty as an adult to do whatever she wanted. She could smoke, drink, and even fall in love with Bill Glass, a young man she met on the First National movie lot. Otto pointed out that Mr. Glass was a nobody, and worse—a Jew. Across town, the Orthodox Glass parents were having their own conniptions over a possible shiksa bride.

Nevertheless, the engagement was duly announced in the papers. Jack's telegram hoping that his "dear Goopher" would be happy only reminded her of the god she had lost and the mere mortal she was getting in his place. A few weeks later she called off the marriage while she was on location in San Antonio filming *The Rough Riders*. Director William Wellman and the cast of *Wings*—Buddy Rogers, the "It Girl" Clara Bow, and Dick Arlen—were also on location there, and Mary enjoyed the incessant partying, fueled by high-quality bootleg booze, that followed each day's shoot.

Mary soon came to realize, if only wryly, that she was more "in love with love," whose affirmations she had tasted so seldom, than with Bill. Truth be told, almost anyone who would take her away from Otto would have seemed incredibly attractive. In fact, Mary was a textbook example of what is taught in Psych 101: A child who has been denied love and affection from her parents is generally going to pursue love in all the wrong places. And since Mary was becoming one of the most beautiful women in Hollywood, she met a lot of men, and, though I hate to say it, made a lot of bad decisions.

MARY (LOWER RIGHT) ON LOCATION OUTSIDE SAN ANTONIO, FRATERNIZES WITH THE CAST OF "WINGS" AFTER HOURS. 1927.

One of them was a man named Ken Hawks. On her return to Hollywood, she visited a friend at Fox and was introduced to an assistant producer. He was all of twenty-six, a good dresser, tall and lean, with "a grin a mile wide." What he did not have, she realized when Ken began wooing her, was much of a sex drive. She forestalled his proposal by confessing her affair with Barrymore, but he found her desire to come clean reassuring. About the rest of that prenuptial period Mary says only that the two of them were wonderfully companionable, whether golfing, going to concerts, or shopping for their future home. And yet some kind of naïveté or denial was at work: "We had some time since decided that anything 'shady' between us had to go, we would play it straight and wait until we were married." Playing at straightness was probably key. But Mary had committed herself, even though she confessed to her diary that Ken "was not a sensual person." On the other hand, marrying him would get her away from Daddy for good.

In 1927 (two months after the opening of the first "talkie," *The Jazz Singer*), Ken Hawks got the long-term contract from Fox he had been praying for. It made him a full director like his older brother, the far more famous Howard Hawks. He and Mary wed

the next year at the hated Temple Hill house. After the ceremonial hoohah, the couple was driven to Union Station to catch the Santa Fe for the first leg of the train ride to New York.

What took place in the sleeper on their wedding night was sweet. Ken tenderly kissed Mary goodnight and climbed to the upper berth.

A few months after returning to Hollywood, Ken's continued lack of interest—he frequently pleaded headaches and chronic intestinal trouble—drove her into an affair with a producer at Fox. She became pregnant almost at once and had an abortion, which was called "therapeutic treatment" by the exclusive facility tricked out for the purpose (fodder for a novel she wrote forty years later, after she joined the Catholic Church and rethought the whole business). No sooner had that blown over—Helen took it on herself to tell Ken about the affair—than the hurricane-force winds of the talkies put Mary's movie career in jeopardy.

She was now under contract to Fox, and like everyone else on the lot was required to go to Movietone to have her voice tested. The primitive sound equipment hardened her contralto, and Sol Wurtzel, who ran the studio, offered Mary a contract for $2,000 a week—half what she'd been making before.

Otto turned it down, and Wurtzel seized the long-awaited opportunity to let him have it on behalf of all the producers who had had to endure that insufferable man's greed and arrogance. In the future, Wurtzel made clear, they would negotiate directly with Mary or an agent, but never again with Otto.

Mary stayed away from the cameras for ten long months, happily learning how to be a good hostess in her new home on Lookout Mountain in the Hollywood Hills. Ken was doing nicely, too. His first assignment as director—*Big Time*, with Mae Clark and Lee Tracy—had turned out well; his next would be with Warner Baxter, Fox's biggest star, about airplane pilots in the Great War. Ken was eager to outdo the aerial footage that William Wellman did for *Wings*. He planned to go up in one of the World War I biplanes to get shots of air battles that would knock the industry for a loop. His recent success in the stock market, this being the giddy 1920s, made him cocky about his decision making, and he felt certain he was headed for cinematic greatness.

At their home two of Mary's favorite dinner guests were the actor Fredric March and his wife, Florence Eldridge. She and the comic actor Edward Everett Horton were about to begin rehearsals for a play that would run for six weeks at the Majestic Theater in Los Angeles, and he offered Mary a part. She jumped at the chance to do comedy and surprised herself by turning in an adroit performance and developing self-confidence onstage. Within a week of opening night she had five offers from studios that had turned her down because they had heard she sounded like a man.

After a Saturday matinee Mary was taking a nap before the evening performance when she became aware that someone was sitting beside her. It was Florence, who looked very serious. Mary couldn't make sense out of what she was saying, but when she heard "there's been an accident," she knew it must have something to do with the dogfight Ken was shooting from a biplane that afternoon. Florence kept saying, "They're not sure about anything yet." But soon they were. The biplane carrying the actors had collided with the one carrying the director and cameraman, ending in a fiery plunge into the Pacific. Ten men died. The film was to have been titled *Such Men Are Dangerous.*

Just When She Thought
Things Couldn't Get Worse

ONSIDERING THE MOCKING TONE Mary used when describing Ken's lack of interest in her, you might have thought his death offered a chance to find real intimacy. But in *My Story* she wrote that she was devastated by her loss, as any young wife would be. Now the young widow, escaped from parents who had made all decisions for her, only to marry a husband who did much the same, was forced to be on her own. With no one to tell her what to do, Mary avoided the need to make decisions by taking sedatives and sleeping . . . sleeping . . . sleeping.

Her gradual recovery took place in the home of Florence and Fredric March. After ten days of loving care from the couple, Mary's crying jags became less frequent, and she was ready to take certain steps. She was determined never to go back to the house she and Ken had shared, not even to get her clothes. When told it would have to be sold for back taxes, she welcomed the news; a sale would at least cover what was owed on the mortgage.

In spite of her parents' tearful exhortations to return home—

"You can come back and be our little girl"—their invitation, like the spider's invitation to the fly, was declined. But Mary had to face the fact that after ten years in movies, during which she had grossed half a million dollars, she had only three thousand dollars in the bank. Of course, there was the Temple Hill house that her earnings had bought, but Otto owned that, and scoffed at the idea of selling it. The two-hundred-thousand-dollar insurance policy on Ken's life had lapsed shortly after he lost everything in the stock market, and there was evidence he'd squandered plenty settling golf, football, and boxing bets.

After moving into a small rented apartment in Hollywood, with an obligatory extra room for a maid, Mary went to work at Paramount for her first talkie, *Ladies Love Brutes*. She'd dropped twenty pounds in the meantime, and the stills from that movie show an emaciated figure. In the course of one scene, Mary again fainted.

Maybe it was the plot. An Italian building contractor, Joe Forziati, with mobster friends, wants to marry a high-society dame, Mimi Howell (Mary), awaiting a divorce from her husband, Dwight Howell. Mary says she has to think of her child and can't marry a man with ties to gangsters. The contractor decides to kidnap the boy and then heroically rescues him. But then . . . well, *Citizen Kane* it wasn't, though it was co-written by Herman Mankiewicz, ten years before he wrote his masterpiece. Whatever caused Mary's swoon, she revived after brandy and a raw egg.

Too exhausted from acting in these preposterous melodramas to socialize in the evenings, Mary stayed home, hoped neither her father nor mother would phone, and kept company with highballs until she fell asleep. She had terrifying dreams of Ken, night after

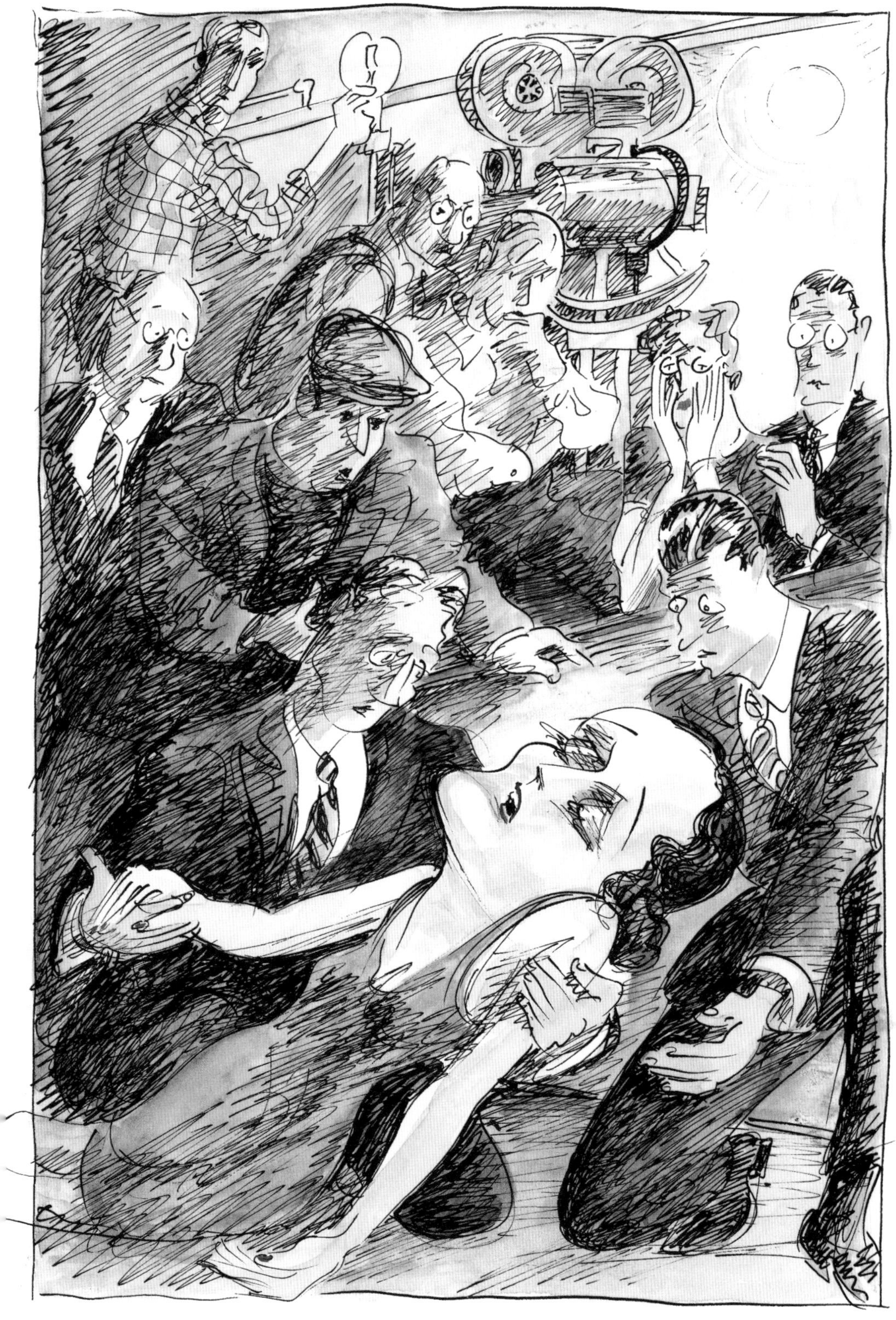

night, usually swimming toward her from the debris of his biplane in the Pacific, trying to reach her and crying for help.

She was all of twenty-three, already widowed, alone and anxious. One morning she awoke to see a patchy rash on her body. On a friend's recommendation, she went to see Dr. Franklyn Thorpe, one of the general practitioners in a Hollywood clinic. He diagnosed her as having returned to acting too soon after the trauma of her husband's death, but later, when her X-rays came back, he said she was also suffering from incipient tuberculosis.

The cost of a sanatorium was too steep, but Mary did promise to follow his regimen at home—sun, a glass of milk every half hour, mineral oil, and lots of bed rest. There were to be no visitors, no phone calls, even worse no cigarettes or liquor. The good doctor dropped in to see her every evening on his way home, however, and soon their conversation became more personal.

Franklyn Thorpe was thirty-six, thirteen years older than Mary and one inch shorter than her five feet six inches, though admittedly good-looking, and with a good head of hair. He had struggled financially to complete his medical degree, and then put in lean years interning. He was currently sharing space, but he dreamed of having his own practice where he would specialize in gynecology and obstetrics. A few months of his strict supervision of Mary's recovery put fifteen pounds on her, and the patient felt fit enough to return to work—even to fall in love again.

Mary's friends advised her to wait. Marian Spitzer, a former reporter for the *New York Globe* and now a screenwriter for Paramount, pleaded with her not to marry just because it was "lousy living alone." When Mary mentioned her intention to help Franklyn set up his own practice after they married, Marian warned her against once again spending all her money. Such advice proved useless. Mary resolved to knuckle down and get Thorpe on his feet professionally, encouraging all her friends to bring him their pelvic business. "Then I could quit work and be a doctor's wife, make him a good home, and have children."

Forty years after my fascination with Mary began, I still cannot fathom her desire to simply play the bourgeois wifey and breed. Did she *really* have no ambition? No respect for her talent or profession? No curiosity to find out what she was capable of? Weeks before she married Thorpe, RKO offered her a contract *strictly for starring roles!* Mary decided against it. Her reasoning: "Once your name goes above the title of a picture it must never come down, or your prestige is gone."

For cryin' out loud! Even if what you say is true, why couldn't you take a chance? Wendy Hiller starred in only three movies before being relegated to supporting roles for the rest of her career, but in those three movies—*Pygmalion* (1938), *I Know Where I'm Going* (1945), and *Major Barbara* (1941)—her radiance is there forever. *Why couldn't you go for greatness? Did you fear you weren't talented enough? Jeezus! All artists have doubts, all artists worry they're just not as good as they should be. Only hacks and one or two geniuses have confidence. You could have been one of the greatest.* Oh, well. Talking to you is like talking to a movie screen. It won't change the ending.

In June of 1931 a jubilant Mary and a mysteriously resigned Franklyn drove down to Yuma, Arizona, where a justice at the courthouse tied the knot. And here's what she wrote in her diary that evening: "It's a beautiful June night, with the moon riding high— and the bridegroom never said a word." Was Franklyn forced into marrying her? If so, why? Was Mary pregnant? Or was it something Mary could not have imagined? According to the 1930 census figures for Los Angeles, he already had a wife, Lillian Lawton Miles, and there is no record of a divorce. Whatever the reason, Thorpe was clearly not thrilled to be married.

I know a little something about being an ambivalent bridegroom. When I was twenty-seven, I became engaged to an attractive woman, my own age, far more competent and worldly than I was. She was also Jewish, which would please my family. Indeed, everything about the match was fine except I had to face the fact that *I didn't really want to marry her.* I decided to call it off with a letter. Once mailed, I thought I was free, but I was not free of guilt. Haunted by the terrible pain I imagined my letter must have caused, I decided to go through with the marriage, convincing myself I was one of those damaged unfortunates incapable of feeling love for *anyone.* It seemed logical then to marry a woman eager to have me.

After we exchanged vows at Temple Rodeph Sholom, on Manhattan's Upper West Side, we went upstairs to where the reception and dinner were to be held (paid for by mother's life savings of $3,000, since my wife's family was even poorer than mine). Many of my friends were there, including my oldest friend, Howard "Fuzzy" Fussiner, and my best man, Milton Glaser, my former partner at Push Pin Studios. There was a three-piece band led by a clarinetist who started playing "The Farmer in the Dell." My friends formed a large circle for dancing, and pushed me in the center. They all began

singing, but when they came to "and the farmer takes a wife, the farmer takes a wife," instead of choosing my bride I chose Fuzzy. Everyone began shouting, "No, Ed, no!! *PICK YOUR BRIDE!!!*" I suddenly understood the choice I was supposed to make, and let go of Fuzzy's arm.

I bet that clarinet player never wearied of telling the story about the world's dumbest bridegroom. Ah, well. Let's get back to that other conflicted bridegroom, Franklyn Thorpe.

I don't know why, but shortly after Thorpe married, and set up his fancy new office, he decided that he and Mary should go to Hawaii for a long holiday. He shut down his practice, learned to sail, bought a schooner and hired a small crew (all with Mary's money), and they took off in May 1932. Their daughter, Marylyn—they effectively named her after themselves—was born on the island in June.

Three months later MGM borrowed Mary from Warner's to appear opposite Clark Gable, without his manicured mustache this time, and Jean Harlow in *Red Dust*. The mise-en-scène was a rubber plantation in French Indochina that compelled everyone to sweat. Under klieg lights and machine-generated rain, the rugged Gable was asked to hold Mary so camera angles could be lined up. After a while his strength gave out, and a stool was fetched to support her bottom. The rain was turned on, and just as the clapper came down the crew burst out laughing—vapor was coming off the stars' heads. After they heated the water, the scene finally got filmed.

That wasn't the only difficulty that plagued the director Victor Fleming. Jean Harlow's husband, the producer Paul Bern, was feckless enough to commit suicide in the middle of production. Mary, for her part, was understandably torn by not being able to be at home caring for her baby. Nevertheless, her convincing portrait of a frigid married woman melted by the dimpled burliness of Gable made the critics single her out for special praise.

The 1932 film was a big hit, and Mary was once again offered a starring contract, this time from Paramount. She declined again, choosing a long-term contract with Warner's that reduced her bargaining position but gave her a good steady income for the next four years. The worsening Depression had everyone in Hollywood searching for financial security. Thanks to the three-month Hawaiian cruise, Franklyn's practice had fallen off. His name was no longer to be found in the gossip columns as "Doctor to the Stars," and the bank where he held most of his money had failed. He and Mary were now forced to live modestly, while Otto was still living in the mansion with two cars and three servants, all paid for by Mary.

At Franklyn's angry insistence, Mary went to have it out with her father and confront him with this proposition: She would give up her one-third right to the property, and he and Helen could have the house, worth $75,000, free and clear. He could sell it, open up a business, or do whatever he wished, but he would not receive any more money from her.

Not only was selling "his" home out of the question for Otto, but he expected Mary to pay for another driveway and a swimming pool. He got a little more money out of her, but when she discovered some of his tricky embezzlements, she stopped all payments. Undeterred, Otto took out a mortgage of $22,500 and built an elaborate swimming pool in the shape of a lagoon, at the astronomical cost of $18,000—in the middle of the Great Depression!

While Mary was rehearsing with Edward G. Robinson on the set of *The Man with Two Faces*, based on the play *The Dark Tower*, by George S. Kaufman and Alexander Woollcott, she was called to the phone. A reporter wanted to know how she planned to answer the suit by her parents. Otto and Helen were suing her for maintenance! Their accusation of nonsupport made the tabloids. At the trial Mary testified, "From 1920 to1930, I gave my father $461,000," while she kept only $24,00. Her lawyer said his client

was willing to pay them $100 a month. Case dismissed. The next day reporters got Otto to pose gazing sadly into the water of his elegant pool, then ran the photo with the caption "Down to their last swimming pool."

Otto, now a laughingstock, put the estate up for sale for $200,000. The best offer he got was for a mere $80,000. Certain—Otto was always certain—that he could get more, he put the house up for auction. The hammer came down at $25,000.

Mary was no longer being ripped off by her parents, but she still had Franklyn to support. His elegant office always seemed to need new equipment. Mary was paying for Nellie, the English nanny for Marylyn, the mortgage on their Toluca Lake home in the San Fernando Valley based on twice its estimated value, and her always à la mode wardrobe. Her salary covered it all, but she worked without any respite from her schedule, referring to a series of films she shot during this period as "the dreary eighteen." Dreary doesn't quite cover it: *The Lost Squadron* of 1932 concerns a Hollywood director (the bald-pated German émigré actor Erich von Stroheim) who risks the lives of airplane stuntmen to get thrills for his picture. Mary plays his unhappy wife, and is required to react to a fireball, just like the one that had killed Ken. Heroically, she somehow got through it.

In 1933 alone she appeared in six movies. When Mary got home after filming, Marylyn was usually asleep, and being alone with Franklyn was more of a strain than being on the set. Like Otto, he had a trigger temper and a talent for enumerating her faults. Mary had had enough. She wanted out. Franklyn didn't. He liked living in the style to which she had accustomed him.

Franklyn knew, of course, that she had had assignations with men since their marriage, and if Mary took legal steps toward a divorce, he would threaten to accuse her of being an unfit mother. Unaware of her husband's own extramarital affairs, Mary went to see her friend Lasher Gallagher, an attorney. He advised her to bide her time. He warned that she would soon be offered mother roles, and a custody trial that besmirched her character would ruin her career. Seeing the distraught state she was in, Gallagher suggested she take a short holiday. He and his wife were on their way to Cuba. Why not fly with them to New York?

As it happened, Mary, for the first time since she had signed up with Warner's, had two weeks free between assignments. *The Kennel*

Murder Case (1933), in which she had second billing to William Powell, was only a week from wrapping up. She really could take off, but she knew Franklyn would fly into one of his screaming rages if she suggested it. When she and her friend Marian Spitzer met for dinner at Musso and Frank's, Mary unburdened herself. After the second martini, Mary mentioned the Gallaghers' coming trip, and how much she would like to go with them as far as New York. It would be so good to get away.

Marian, who had warned Mary not to marry Franklyn in the first place, now became her backbone, insisting she stand up to her controlling husband once and for all and take a flier to New York. Marian had an army of friends there who would be only too happy to squire her beautiful and talented friend all over town. Wishing to be helpful, Marian would write her good friends Bennett Cerf and George S. Kaufman. She assured Mary that both Cerf, the dynamic thirty-five-year-old publisher of Random House, and Kaufman, the celebrated forty-three-year-old Broadway playwright, would welcome the chance to show her the town. And knowing of their appreciation of beautiful women, Marian suggested that they would undoubtedly desire being more than mere tour guides.

But wasn't Kaufman married? Marian explained that it was an "open" marriage. Beatrice Kaufman had had a stillbirth, and after that it was said she wouldn't sleep with George. While he and Beatrice continued to reside genially in their luxurious apartment on Central Park West, both saw other people. George dallied in his studio on the east side of Central Park; his wife used the Plaza.

Needless to say, they were discreet, Mary was told, although George always had some new beauty close at hand, usually an actress or a chorus girl. Marian closed her résumé of Kaufman by quoting Max Gordon, the playwright's frequent producer, who had once described him as a "male nymphomaniac." Cerf, Mary knew from reading gossip columns, was quite the ladies' man, and *he* was still a bachelor.

After this dish on just two of the men she would meet in New York, Mary found the strength to tough out Franklyn's predictable tirade when she announced she *would* take a break. After all, it was her labor that kept him living high on the hog, and little Marylyn would be in good hands with Nellie. Never a gracious loser, Franklyn refused to bring their daughter to the airport to see her mother off. Mary kissed her goodbye at home as the taxi waited.

Mary Goes to New York and Meets the Man of Her Dreams

PLAINLY MARY WAS GOING to New York to have an affair. At least that's my take. Of course, she didn't put it so baldly in *My Story*—by the 1950s when she wrote her autobiography she had a television career as a matron to protect. Remember, too, that both Cerf and Kaufman were still alive when her memoir was published in 1959, so she had to be circumspect about what she revealed about them, as well as about herself.

Cursed with the world's foremost fixation on Mary Astor, I had to know more about what happened during that trip than the bowdlerized version she presented in her memoir. Where did she and George first meet? How did they become lovers? Did he gossip about his friends? Was the pillow talk frisky? Like that. But how could that be accomplished without actually talking to the long-dead actress? *I decided the only thing to do was to channel her in her Catholic heaven.*

I was certain such an enclave existed, but I had no idea how to reach her there. I went to my old friend Neil Hickey, a Catholic, and asked him whether he'd ever contacted anyone in heaven. "Are you kidding?" he snapped. "I can barely deal with cyberspace." But when I explained that it was imperative I speak to Mary Astor, he called up —— and made an appointment for me. Neil said I should address the man as Monsignor.

Monsignor —— at first was suspicious of my request to meet Mary. I explained that far from intending to ridicule Miss Astor I adored her, and was simply trying to fill in some blank spots in the bio I was writing. I assured him I would confine my questions to 1933 and not inquire about her life in the hereafter. He said he would grant me fifteen minutes on condition I not name him or the particular archdiocese in my acknowledgments. I gave him my word.

I waited for Mary in a small, dimly lit room adjacent to the Monsignor's office, expecting a woman of eighty-two, which is how old she was when she died. I liked the idea that she would now be four years younger than I was. We'd now have our aches and pains in common, I figured.

Suddenly I felt a great draft, and looked up to see the narrow Gothic windows burst open, making way for an ethereal flying figure with great legs. The twenty-seven-year-old knockout who pulled to a halt before me wore a bemused smile. She was taller than I expected, but then again I'm old now and have lost two inches.

In that familiar mellow voice she said, "Monsignor thought that since you were going to quiz me about 1933, you should see me as I was then." When I addressed her as "Miss Astor," she asked me to call her Mary. I'm sorry to report that she's still a heavy smoker. Or

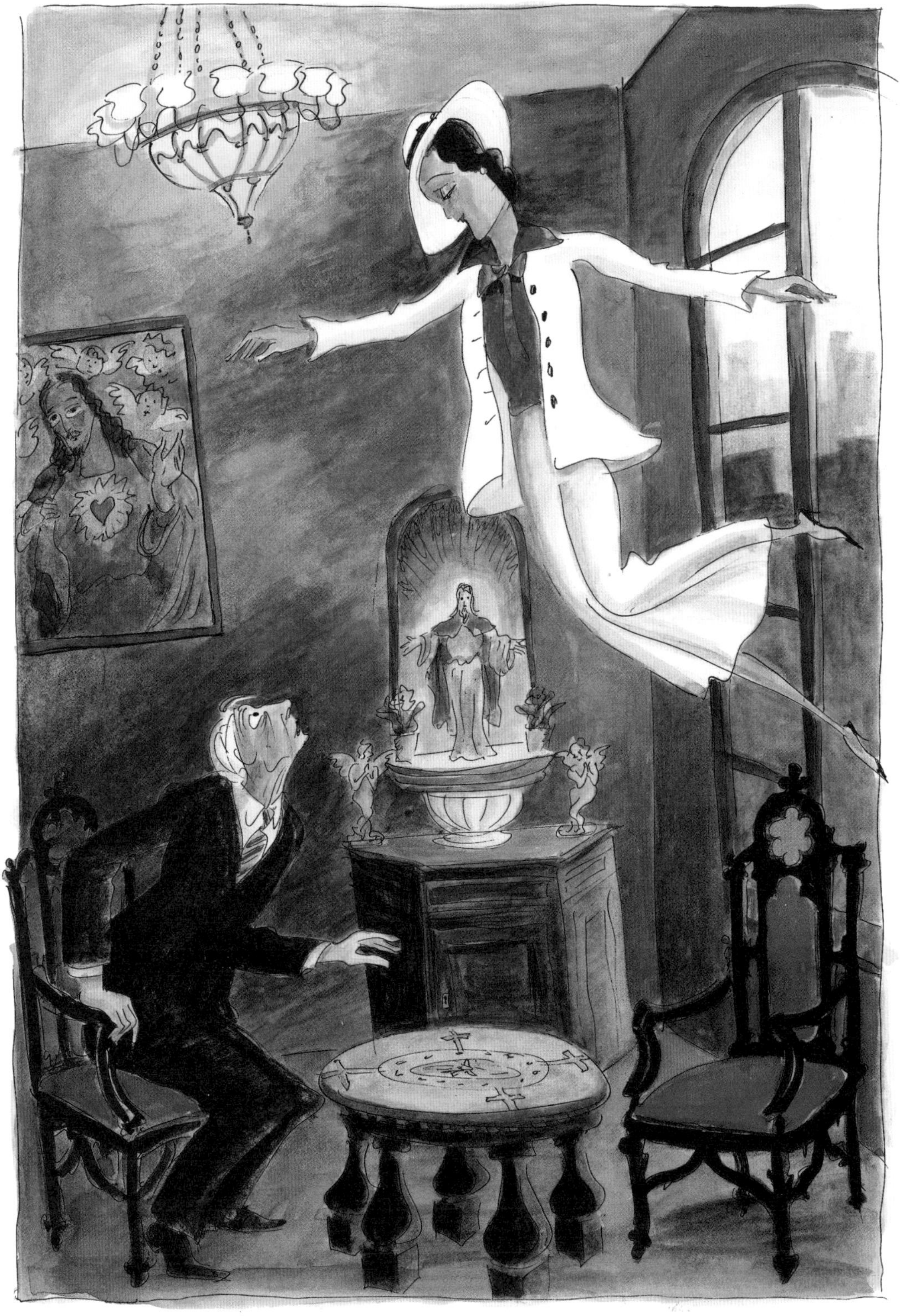

maybe that was part of reappearing as she was that year. Come to think of it, the pack of Lucky Strike cigarettes she held was green, as Lucky's were before the war.

Mary's diction was exactly as described by her friends, who noted the split between her classy elocution and sassy tongue. The actor David Niven remembered his surprise at hearing a longshoreman's vocabulary coming from a woman who "looked like a beautiful and highly shockable nun." She used few expletives with me, however. Having been told that I had a thing about her, maybe she didn't want to disenchant me with too many zingers. Or maybe she was just being deferential to my white hair.

"Shall we begin, Ed?" she asked.

You mean, like now? Well, sure—uh, before your 1933 trip, when was the last time you'd been in New York?

Not since 1928, when I was on my honeymoon with Ken—though no honey was actually exchanged, as you know. By '33 the city was enormously different. Men were selling apples everywhere, and many of the elegant stores had gone belly-up. Those bronze traffic towers in the middle of Fifth Avenue were gone. Only the cabs looked prosperous—they were beamier and more comfy, and each fleet had a different color combination. Oh—and women's hats had changed. The cloche was out; foreheads were back.

Where did you stay when you arrived?

I had a suite at the Ambassador on Park and Fifty-First. Most Hollywood types at the time stayed at the newer Waldorf-Astoria, one block south, where the press hung out, hoping to spot stars. I didn't want that scene, though I liked being recognized by people on the street and in stores. Fans were courteous then, not overfamiliar and predatory, like later. It bucked me up.

Anyway, when I arrived, an extravagant floral arrangement was waiting for me—a come-on from the overly eager Bennett Cerf. He threw a party in my honor and lent me a pirated copy of *Ulysses*, which he was about to get permission to publish. I already had my own pirated copy and had read it, so when he propositioned me the following night I said, "No, I won't—no." [laughs] He didn't get it. But we did go dancing at El Morocco, the place to be seen then, along with the Stork Club. Bennett was good-looking in a boyish kind of way, and he was tall enough, but his serial joke telling was a chemistry killer.

Where did you first meet Kaufman, and what did you think?

George was out of town when I first arrived, but he finally phoned, and we planned to meet up on the weekend. Friday I was having lunch at the Algonquin with a female friend, and who walked in but George, who knew her. He came over at once and she introduced him. Not exactly a Barrymore, you know, but tall and gracious. He had a nose like this [gestures], heavy framed glasses and a pompadour of black wavy hair—very "Jewish-looking," my father would have said. But I found him attractive.

What was your first date?

George retrieved me on Saturday in a dark green Packard—his chauffeur, that is; George didn't drive. We went to the Central Park Casino, close to his apartment on Central Park

West. The Casino was a real Victorian beauty of the time, but it was soon to be razed by LaGuardia and his urban planner—they didn't like having a rich man's club in a public park. The Casino dance orchestra was led by Eddy Duchin, who was movie-star handsome, and had a nice touch on the piano, but George was no cheek-to-cheeker—my god, he wasn't even a hand-shaker, he was so phobic. He barely ate, and just kept compulsively crumbing the table—he was full of tics. Not this kid: I ate a whole lobster, and washed it down with a couple of daiquiris. Prohibition was as good as over, and even city-owned restaurants paid no attention. George hardly drank; he said Jews couldn't afford not to know what was going on. [laughs]

Well, what did you talk about?

We had Hollywood friends in common, of course—that was an icebreaker. Then he pretended to believe I really was an Astor, asking earnestly about the old family beaver trade until I stopped him by telling about my audition for Lasky, and how I got the name. I always wondered whether my name was why producers so often cast me as a high-society dame. . . . George was appalled to learn how little control I had over my career, and told me I should mix in theater with work in pictures. No idle gallantry there; he was dead serious. Lord, what a dope I was, always holding out for the steady paycheck—just no guts at all. How could he stand it? Well, he liked to succeed, and he was always a big success with me. He knew I genuinely got off on him—in all senses, as it turned out.

So what happened next?

We went to the Music Box on Forty-Fifth Street to see Victor Moore and William Gaxton do their stuff in *Of Thee I Sing*, which was already having a strong revival. The show had Ira Gershwin's wittiest lyrics. George—my George, not his brother—never liked the sentimental stuff, and in that show there was only one song with a melody that grabbed you, "Who Cares?" I crumple whenever I hear it. It's the only song in that show that people still sing.

Then we caught the second act of Cole Porter's *Gay Divorce* at the Schubert. When it was later made into a movie, the Hays Office made them change the title to *The Gay Divorcee*, because a divorce must never be gay, my dear. That was the first time I saw Fred Astaire in the flesh, if you can call him corporeal. I was spellbound watching him in "Night and Day," but then I realized George was watching me the same way. And he was a pro, you know, so it felt good.

Did either of you talk about your marriages?

I never spoke of Franklyn, apart from mentioning the time he invited me to watch him perform a hysterectomy. I could tell George thought I was insane, and looking back at our custody battle it does seem a little premonitory. George never mentioned Beatrice, either, though I terribly wanted to know how an open marriage worked, having had the shut kind myself. I did know they'd adopted a little girl, so that bound them. And Bea was fun as all get-out, apparently— guys like Harpo Marx and Noël Coward were crazy about her. She was chic, too—a pioneer pants-wearer. Plump-ish, but attractive. In fact she was getting her own about town. She wanted a good time. That's probably what came between them—that wasn't really George's thing. When he wasn't getting laid, he had a hard-on for anxiety. Poor Ed—does that put you off?

Don't worry about it.

Anyway, it came out that our daughters were the same age, but I didn't want to hear about George as a doting papa. Remember, I'd been supporting mine since childhood.

George took you to meet the Algonquin tribe. How was it?

Mixed. I confess I was nervous about how they'd react to a vulgarian from Hollywood. I knew that Bea was sometimes there, on her own steam, whereas I was never a bon-mot maker. I was just a looker. Sure they were witty, but a lot of it was forced. Not Benchley—he was a doll. And Heywood Broun was capable of gravity, which offered a kind of tragic relief. But he really did look like an unmade bed. I forget what paper his column appeared in.

In 1933 it was the *World-Telegram*. How did Dorothy Parker treat you?

She was sweet. Not yet a confirmed bitch—though I do remember her referring to MGM as "Metro-Goldwyn-Merde." Only Edna Ferber seemed chilly. She loved George, I was told, and had a horse face, so I understood her hostil-ity. George had great respect for her as a collaborator after they wrote *Dinner at Eight*, but he had little to do with her socially. It was Moss Hart who took her everywhere. He liked to be seen with the woman who had written *Show-boat*, and apparently he used her as a beard at parties while he scouted for young men.

Really? I didn't know that. Looking back, what was the high point of that trip?

Well, the narrative starts to smoke a little bit here. You okay with that?

I think I can handle it.

One night early on we went to see *Run, Little Chillun*. It was a New Deal thing, an all-Negro production. The dancing and music were disinhibiting, no question, although George had already kissed me in the cab. We messed around during the first two acts, and my hand left my lap during the third. It had been years since I'd felt up a man in public, and I came close to putting him on the spot. [laughs] Afterwards we had a drink someplace, and then went to a little flat he kept on East Seventy-Third Street, where we could finally be alone.

So . . . what kind of lover is a germ freak?

I did ask him once how he could bear to kiss me, given how it was apt to involve moisture; he said I was worth the risk. George liked his sex the way he liked bridge: he was no spectator—he was in or he was out. Mostly he was in, and a perfect fit he was too. And the stamina! I snapped back pretty fast myself in those days, but George was a phenomenon. Another time, when he "fucked the living daylights out of me until four a.m. and I was half dead"—some of what the papers published as the diary was forged, but I'm

75

the divorce rate. He suggested changing it to "I'll be loving you Thursday."

I decided I was his Girl Thursday—if that. But I wasn't going to risk losing what I had. I cut the love talk and made it clear I'd accept our affair on any terms. The evening I left we had dinner again at "our" 21—one of the most delightful speakeasies in the city. When we went to it a year later, after Prohibition had been repealed, it seemed suddenly rather staid, but I still loved it.

Of course, my little holiday came to an end far too soon. George's chauffeur drove us to North Beach Airport—LaGuardia, as it became—and he kissed me goodbye. That sounds perfunctory, but it must have meant something, because George normally couldn't stand kissing in public.

One thing that occurs to me: If I had managed to stay with George, would I still have become an alcoholic, or would he have gotten me into therapy that much earlier? No telling. But if I'd gone into the Church, as I ultimately did, he'd have thrown me out anyway. And face it, Ed—so would you.

You're probably right. I only suspend disbelief when I'm in a theater. But before we part, you should know that I'm not the only man obsessed with you. And even lots of more credible people hold you in high regard as a great screen presence, and as a superb actress.

You're dear, Ed, but you really ought to get out more. You're too pale, too—I bet you spend too much time indoors watching old movies.

Hell Hath No Fury like a
Cuckold Scorned

MARY FLEW BACK to Los Angeles on the same DC-1 airplane she had taken to New York. It had to be the same plane because Douglas Aircraft produced only one model of the DC-1 before it added improvements that led to the DC-2 and DC-3. As a model plane builder from the time I was ten, I took an enormous interest in air travel. I knew all about the DC-1. It was the first twin-engine all-metal monoplane (wooden wings for passenger airliners had been outlawed), and it could take off, fly, and land with one dysfunctional engine. The DC (**D**ouglas **C**ommercial) plane that TWA began flying on July 1, 1933, was the first one to go nonstop between Los Angeles and New York, making the journey in just thirteen hours and five minutes, a new record.

What the DC-1 could not do was go faster than the speed of light, which is what Mary needed to get back to the Warner set on time, but she wanted one more night with George, and damn the consequences. I like to imagine her sitting in the twelve-passenger

plane—head back, eyes closed, and smiling all the way west with the same gone expression on her face that she wore in *Red Dust* after getting down with Clark Gable. What I can't imagine is how she behaved with Thorpe when she returned home. How does one go back to purgatory after tasting paradise?

Warner's kept her so busy after her return that it wasn't until January 1934 that she found time to tell her diary what had happened. "I did meet a man, professional, somewhat older and rather well-to-do, only his first initial is G. and I fell like a ton of bricks— as only I can fall—it was just one of those things . . . that was six months ago and it's still good—we write to each other often, about every two weeks—flowers and telegram for Christmas and New Years; once when Franklyn was away he called me long distance and we talked for half an hour—his last letter finished with 'Think of me my darling, because I certainly think of you.'"

Judging by Mary's diary entry on October 1, she must have managed another trip to New York in 1933. "I am still in a haze—nice rosy glow. It is beautiful, glorious—and I hope it's my last love—can't top it with anything in my experience—nor do I want to."

It was another G-whiz idyll. She saw more rehearsals, "and I saw George—I saw George. Only ten days, but enough to remember the rest of my life—We went to '21'—Our '21'; we drove through the park; we heard a Gilbert and Sullivan operetta, *Ruddigore*—We dined at the Colony; we saw *Life Begins at 8:40*; we saw a movie on Sunday night; we went to Reuben's; we talked and laughed and spent lovely nights at the Essex House."

For the benefit of out-of-towners: Reuben's Restaurant was a particular favorite of Jewish comedians, many of whom, like Jack Benny and Eddie Cantor, were caricatured on its menu. Sadly, it no longer exists, but the Colony Club does. It's still on Park Avenue and Sixty-Second Street, where the club's building, designed by Stanford White, now enjoys landmark status. It remains a social club for rich ladies who lunch; men may dine there as guests, while the Essex House, a luxury hotel, still stands on Central Park South.

I was there only once. In July of 2000 the *New Yorker* magazine succeeded in getting a reservation for me at "Alain Ducasse at the Essex House." The editor, David Remnick, gave me a double-page spread to write and illustrate what it was like to dine in this new restaurant.

It wasn't the food that intrigued but the price. Dinner for one, not including wine, averaged even then between $150 and $225.

My wife, Nancy, who took her Quakerism seriously, had no interest in going there with me. "People don't go there to eat," she said. "They go there to show how much money they can afford to throw away." (Pretty much the same reason Thorsten Veblen gave for why rich people gamble: not to win, but to show the world how much money they could lose and still keep smiling.) Instead, I took Dorothy Gallagher, our closest friend, who I figured would enjoy a good scoff.

The wooden doors to the restaurant looked to be two stories high, as if imported from Kublai Khan's palace. Waiting until it opened for lunch, we nervously checked our appearance in the mirror to make sure we looked worthy. Noon came and we were ushered to our table. The place was certainly opulent, and the dishes would photograph well, but I've had food at the Automat I enjoyed more. Everything brought to us was presented as if it were a rare, exotic offering. The final preposterous flourish was the presentation of the credit card bill: the waiter held a four-foot-long board with about twenty different pens for me to choose from. I'm happy to report the restaurant went the way of all flash, and closed in a couple of years.

Essex House that autumn of 1933 was just one stop on Mary's itinerary. George took her everywhere. As her diary makes clear, she was extremely grateful to have found a tour guide whose attentions did not end at sundown. How can any man help being envious of rich, witty, urbane, talented, indefatigable George? Reading such entries from Mary's diary as "We shared our fourth climax at dawn" can really put a guy's joint out of joint.

But oddly enough, this twentieth-century Casanova was still a virgin when he married at the age of twenty-seven. Three of the four biographies written about GSK all attest to the fact that he and a handful of high school buddies made a pact to remain celibate until they married. George stuck to his pledge. It may not have been that difficult. Beyond the nose and glasses combo that looked as if he'd bought the set from a novelty shop, his behavior was odd.

He vacillated between bursts of rapid speech and long silences. When he was about to face some death-defying task, like taking an elevator to an upper floor in a skyscraper, he would audibly talk to himself to get the courage to forge ahead. This edginess, together with his tall, thin frame, was one of the reasons he would be rejected for the army—and his klutzy gait made him utterly resistible. But when Beatrice Barkow was stuck with him on a blind date, she quickly realized he was a man of superior intelligence. In 1917, a year after meeting, they were wed in Rochester, New York, where the bride's family lived.

You've already read that George and Beatrice had an open marriage, but it's not clear what led to that arrangement. We know their two-room suite in the dingy, long-gone Majestic Hotel on West Seventy-Second Street was furnished with twin beds. One biography of GSK asserts that from the beginning Beatrice found intercourse with George painful, and when her pregnancy produced a stillborn baby, she declined further relations. But another life of the playwright suggests George was so traumatized by what happened that he was rendered impotent with his wife. Take your choice.

In any case it's clear that Beatrice was plenty capable of enjoying dalliances with other men, and that George, easily or reluctantly, adjusted to becoming a ladies man par excellence. They were, nevertheless, utterly devoted to each other. Such an anomaly was difficult for Mary to grasp, so she let herself believe she could win him away.

Mary's diary entries describing her days and nights with George during the first year of their affair read like the breathless gushing of a teenager who has run away from home. At some point even Mary seemed to tumble to the silliness of her romantic certainties. In a later moment of rueful self-analysis she wrote, "How I've ever been able to write all those things I don't know. . . . 'Love of My Life'—'Enduring,' 'Sense of Something Important'—Piffle! Could write in detail about this last trip and seeing George—about the ecstasy contained in a few beautiful hours, but if I did I'd laugh myself sick—I've said it all before—I've felt it all before. . . . Does this happen over and over and over again? If it does it's all a lousy trick. Am I going to keep on forever thinking this is it? What the hell is it and what do I want?"

In spite of such fleeting self-awareness, when she learned that George was going to Palm Springs to work with Moss Hart on a new play, Mary wangled an invitation from Dorothy and Richard Rodgers, who had a home there. All her nights with George, we can assume, made the earth move and littered the lawn with coconuts. Mary's interlude under the palms was followed a few months later by more memorable nights on East Seventy-Third Street. Mary sat in on rehearsals of Kaufman and Hart's *Merrily We Roll Along*. George had wanted her for the lead, and for once Mary had a spark of ambition to go for it, but Warner's refused, and she caved. In this case it was just as well. The play opened in September, and the critics panned it for reasons suggested by Mankiewicz's précis of the plot:

Here's this playwright who writes a play and it's a big success. Then he writes another play and it's a big hit too. All his plays are big successes. All the actresses in them are in love with him, and he has a yacht and a beautiful home in the country. He has a beautiful wife and two beautiful children, and he makes a million dollars. Now the problem that the play propounds is this: How did the poor son of a bitch ever get in this jam?

Mary's happiness in New York contrasted sharply with her misery in Hollywood, chained to second-rate scripts. It was also unbearable to live with a foul-tempered despot after teddy bear George. When Franklyn adamantly refused to give Mary a divorce, she went and rented a small house on Tower Road in Beverly Hills. She told Franklyn that if he wouldn't leave, she and Marylyn would move out.

Unfortunately her husband had anticipated just such a maneuver. Months earlier Franklyn had searched for and found the diary he knew Mary kept. In it he read that his sexual performance was lame, his name-dropping and social climbing offensive, and his profligacy with her hard-earned money infuriating. She even ridiculed him for growing a mustache identical to Clark Gable's, after the star and Franklyn had become skeet-shooting buddies. More important, he read that "G," in New York, was her ideal match. It wasn't hard to figure out who G was—he'd taken her to all the rehearsals and plays of George S. Kaufman.

In the ugly scene following Mary's threat to leave, Thorpe brought her up short. He warned his wife that if she ever tried to walk out he would use the diary's salacious contents to ruin her career and take custody of four-year-old Marylyn. He taunted her by repeating from memory passages describing her ecstasy with other men. If she wanted to dissolve the marriage, it would have to be on his terms.

Mary knew her diary contained not only devastating material about her own life but also secrets about others. If it became public, many lives would be ruined, not just hers. Terrified and at a loss as to what to do, she felt her life collapsing around her.

Franklyn's rage and willingness—no, *eagerness*—to destroy her life drained Mary of all her strength. How could she have been so stupid? Bourbon didn't make her forget, but it did get her to sleep at night; she hoped she'd never wake up.

The next day she asked Franklyn what it would take to end their marriage. His answer: Marylyn, the house, and just about every cent of the $60,000 she had in the bank. Once again she agreed to everything. While they would share Marylyn, legally he would have full custody. In 1935 Mary and her daughter moved to Beverly Hills, and Franklyn won an uncontested divorce.

For a while mother and daughter were happy living in the little house on Tower Road. Mary felt she'd been let out of quarantine. But then the lease expired just as she was ordered away on a shoot in Lake Tahoe. She left Marylyn with Nellie, who was still taking care of the Toluca Lake house for Franklyn. On location the cast got snowed in and everyone got the flu; one man died. Mary was rushed back to Los Angeles in an ambulance with pneumonia. Franklyn was forced to recognize it would be best for Marylyn if her mother, once recovered, moved back to Toluca Lake. Nellie would stay with Marylyn while Mary toiled in front of the cameras. He would take a small place in town.

Mary had little time to savor the sane turn of events. She had signed a new two-year contract with Columbia that meant unrelenting work on a series of B pictures. Their very titles announced their low pedigree: *And So They Were Married*, *Trapped by Television*, and *Lady from Nowhere*. She worked on three or four at a time, which meant retakes on one, costume fittings for two others, and publicity shots for those near release. They weren't "released"—as the old gag went—they escaped.

Further dividing her few hours with Marylyn, Mary took part in the Hollywood fight for a union, a struggle that finally gave birth to the Screen Actors Guild. Among the other organizers was Ann Harding, with whom Mary had appeared in *Holiday*, one of her first talkies. Mary told her former costar why she'd had to give up custody and how she dreaded that if Franklyn ever decided to move away from California with Marylyn, there would be nothing she could do about it. Harding suggested she talk to Roland Rich Woolley, a lawyer who had gotten her out of a similar mess.

Woolley, a Mormon from Utah, was no stranger to clients with scandalous sex lives. As a young lawyer in the 1920s, he had represented Aimee Semple McPherson. The glamorous evangelist who owned her own church and radio station had run off for a tryst with one of her employees, later telling a wild story about having been kidnapped. She was charged with perjury, but Woolley got her acquitted. Now he was almost as famous as the stars he represented. Mary found him friendly and understanding, but he flinched when he heard details about the diary. Still, after mulling it over, he told Mary he thought he could keep it from being entered into evidence. Marylyn had been living with her for a year and was thriving. Woolley suggested Mary sue for custody.

Mary was exhilarated by this encouragement, but she had one misgiving. She had just heard that Sam Goldwyn wanted to borrow her from Columbia to play the role of Edith Cortright in *Dodsworth*, based on the Sinclair Lewis novel. It would be the role of a lifetime. The great director William Wyler, already credited with *Counselor at Law*, starring her old friend John Barrymore, and *The Good Fairy*, with Margaret Sullavan, would now be directing *her*, and the cast would include such notables as Walter Huston and Ruth Chatterton. What if her custody battle popped up on the court calendar right in the middle of filming? Woolley assured her the case could take a year to come up. *Dodsworth* would be in the can by then.

The brief Woolley filed with the court stated that Mary had been blackmailed into signing over custody of her daughter because of her husband's threat to make public the contents of her diary. Furthermore, it claimed Thorpe's marriage to Mary was illegal, since he was already married to a Lillian Miles at the time. And Woolley had Mary's testimony that Franklyn had smacked Marylyn around.

Thorpe's attorney, Joseph Anderson, countered that Mary was an unfit mother and included her diary entry for February 6, 1935, as proof of her depraved character: "I am such a muddle-headed person that I love to tie myself down—my thoughts down—so that they won't go skittering off in all directions. Then, too, maybe Marylyn some day would like to know what sort of person her mother was and maybe she will be consoled when she makes mistakes and gets into jams to know that mother was a champion at making mistakes. . . . I have been and am such a fool. Marylyn, never admit anything to anybody. Honesty is not the best policy."

While these lawyers' briefs were worming their way through the bureaucratic labyrinth of the Superior Court of Los Angeles, Mary was beguiled by her first day on the lot. Wyler greeted her charmingly and said the role would change her career. Also on hand was Huston, who had starred in the title role on Broadway, and

Chatterton, who was to play Dodsworth's spoiled, middle-aged wife who feared getting old. Goldwyn himself appeared on the set to wish everyone good luck.

Many thought Goldwyn a complete idiot, but the playwright Sidney Howard had hard evidence to support his belief. Years earlier he had urged the producer to buy *Dodsworth*—it was only $20,000—and Howard offered to write the script. The producer declined. So Howard adapted it for the stage, and it became a smash. *Now* Goldwyn had to have it—for $160,000. When Howard teased him, the former Samuel Goldfish, née Schmuel Gelbfisz, said he'd actually been canny to wait: "This way I bought a successful play. Before it was only a novel."

As he once famously said, "I'm not always right, but I'm never wrong."

Day after day, Mary laid down one of her best performances. After work she would sometimes meet with Woolley to talk about what his strategy would be at the trial. On one visit he had to break the unhappy news that the case had come up on the court calendar sooner than he expected: July 27.

Dodsworth was still weeks away from completion. When Goldwyn got wind of the news, he tried to get the trial pushed back, but all of Sam's lawyers and all of Sam's flacks couldn't get it postponed. The judge did allow one accommodation: the trial would be held at night.

With a date set, Franklyn began leaking snippets from the diary to the press, and the closer the trial came, the more he fabricated entries for reporters to pant over. He said Mary's confessions included a racy scorecard that listed all the men she had gone to

bed with along with numerical ratings of their prowess. Panic rose in the offices of the major producers. What if one of their macho stars had gotten a zero for the old in-and-out?

Mary's worried attorney read the tabloids and asked her whether there were going to be any more surprises at the trial. Mary swore the revelations were bogus. Woolley believed her, confident that any entry Thorpe had doctored would render the diary inadmissible in court.

The diary itself was presumed to be safely under lock and key in the office of Thorpe's lawyer. Had Woolley known that Florabel Muir was in town to cover the trial, he might well have worried. Muir was one of the New York *Daily News'* top reporters, and arguably the most unethical one on its staff. Since the 1920s she had kidnapped witnesses, bribed law clerks, and broken into offices to rifle desks. Once she got hold of Mary's diary long enough to photograph it, she had no compunctions about making the contents juicier or, if *too* juicy, more printable for the newspapers.

Because of the night sessions and the time difference between coasts, the *News* would be stuck with yesterday's breaking story. To counter this handicap, Florabel phoned in her transcript of the diary. The evening edition, dated Tuesday, July 28, came out just hours before the trial got under way in Los Angeles, and contained Mary's affair with the mysterious "G." Muir never said whom she had bribed to get the diary, but years later she did say she had paid $300. She had offered the lawyer Anderson $5,000; he had turned it down.

The trial was now Big News, and every newspaper editor quickly sent his top reporters to cover it. Since spectators would be pouring into the courtroom, it was changed to the large one on the twenty-first floor of the Los Angeles Superior Court Building; the jury box could be used for overflow press. Judge Goodwin Knight would preside alone. Woolley phoned Mary to arrange a meeting place. He wasn't going to let her face that mob by herself.

The circus was scheduled to start at 7:00 p.m. As Mary was leaving the *Dodsworth* soundstage to meet her attorney, Ruth Chatterton stopped her to ask whether she would have anyone with her in court—"I mean someone to sit in the front row, someone you know is on your team and can give you a wink of encouragement."

Mary laughed. "No, there's no one like that."

Ruth took her hand. "May I drive you down and be with you?"

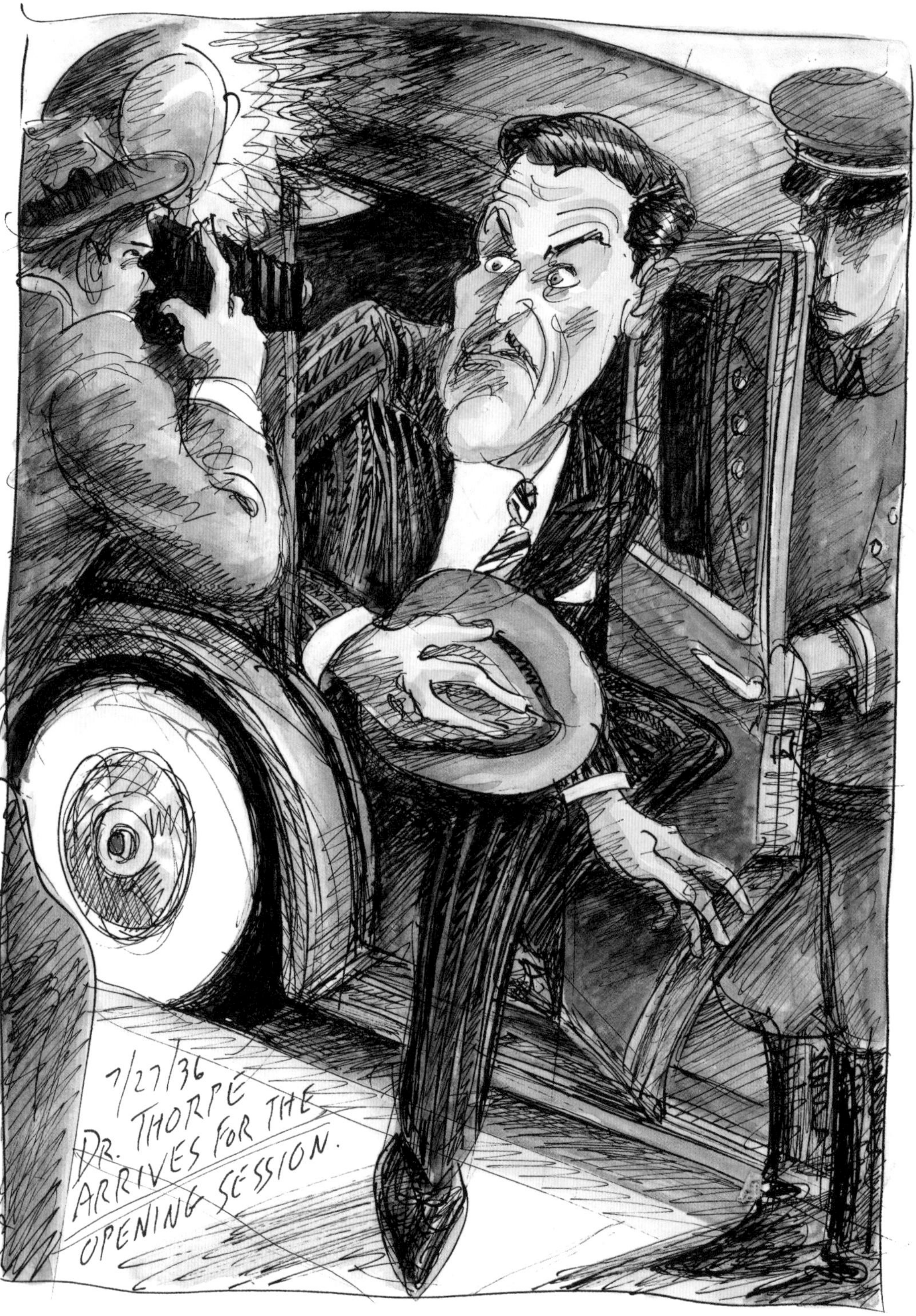
7/27/36
DR. THORPE
ARRIVES FOR THE
OPENING SESSION.

The Trial,
Act I

⸙

ORD THAT THE *Daily News* had somehow obtained and published a transcript of her diary left Mary traumatized. The worst had happened. All of Woolley's promises to keep the diary secret were now meaningless. As Chatterton drove her to the courthouse on Monday, July 27, Mary shared her fears for the future. She stood to lose not only her child but her livelihood. Goldwyn could use the morality clause in her contract to dump her, and get someone else to redo the *Dodsworth* scenes already filmed. There were rumors that the heads of studios were pressuring Goldwyn to get her to drop the suit: they feared the morning headlines could be just the beginning of more shocking revelations—fabricated or not, but once again stigmatizing Hollywood as a godless Gomorrah and prompting another Hearst purification campaign.

William Randolph Hearst, who owned twenty-eight newspapers in eighteen major cities from coast to coast, never missed an opportunity to headline the scandalous sex lives of Hollywood stars to build up his papers' circulation. Although Mary didn't mention it to Chatterton, she knew that sooner or later Hearst and everyone else would find out the identity of "G" in her diary. Her nitwit diary, she realized, could not only ruin her but also drag down the man she deeply loved.

Woolley was pleased to see Chatterton with his client. A celebrated, serious actress sitting in the front row would show the judge that respectable people believed in Mary's character. With a friend on one side and her lawyer on the other, Mary made it through the gauntlet of flashbulbs and reporters shouting questions.

In a roped-off area on the twenty-first floor stood those who had come too late to get a seat. Their only reward that day would be a quick glimpse of Mary Astor in a wide-brimmed black hat and black dress gliding into the courtroom, dressed as if for her own funeral. The spectators, mostly women wearing last year's hat fashion, turned to stare at the solemn, elegant face. Many were devout movie fans who remembered Mary from when she was Barrymore's seventeen-year-old inamorata in *Beau Brummel.* Close to thirty now, she was still beautiful, with auburn hair, an angelic face, and pensive blue eyes. She was always so refined, so ladylike on the

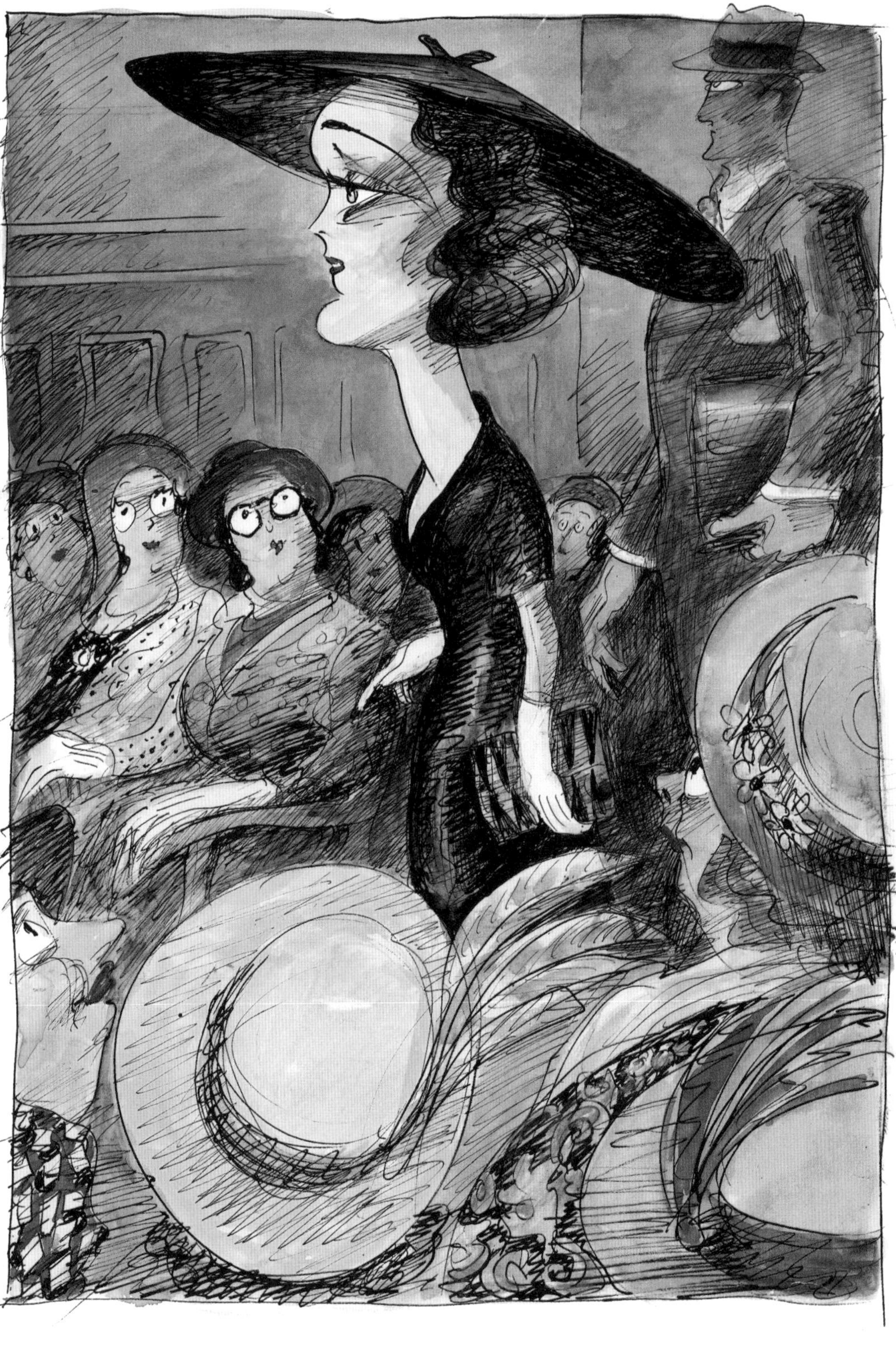

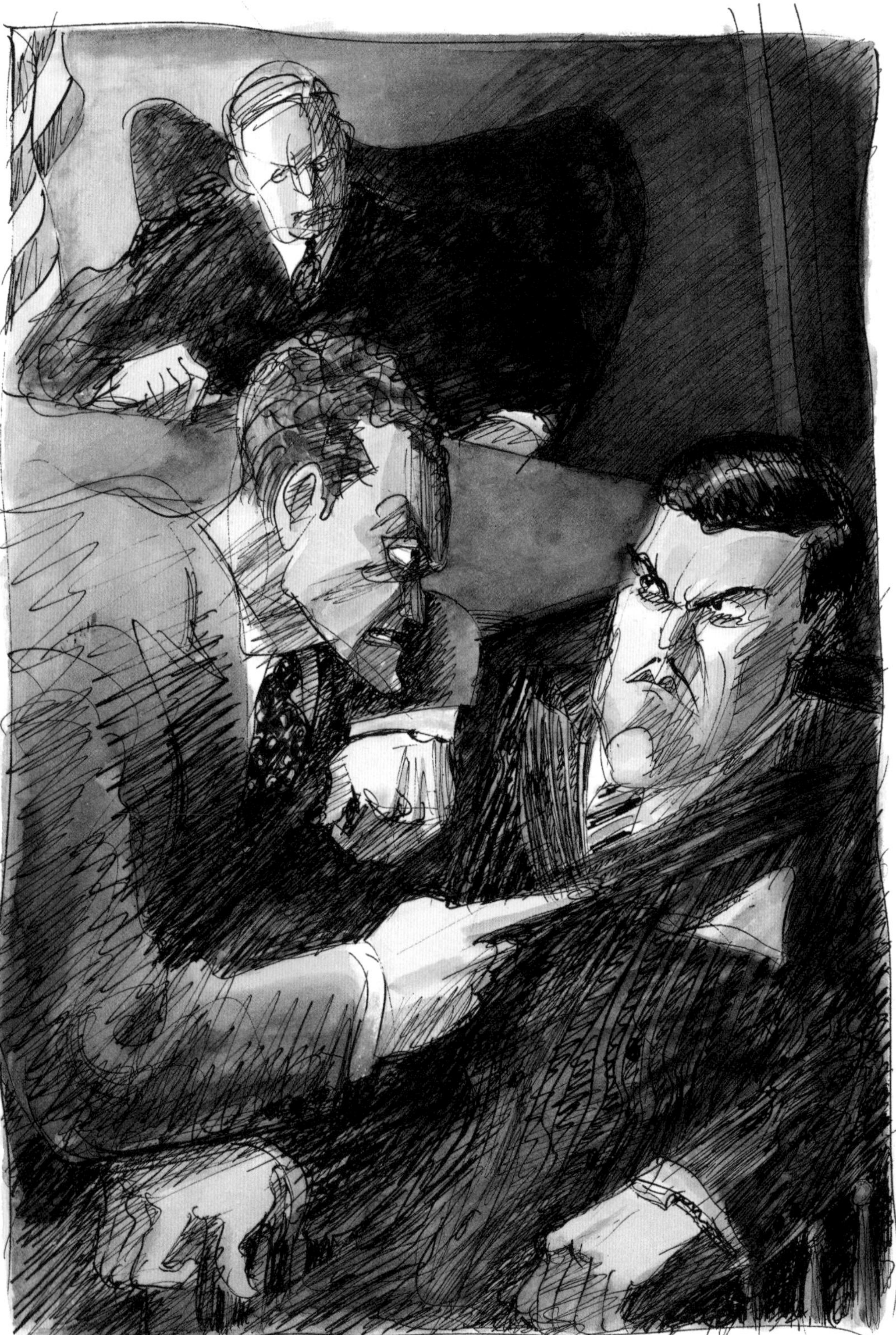

screen—it was hard to believe what the newspapers were saying about her—even the *New York Times.*

The lucky audience in the front row recognized Chatterton and respectfully made a space for her. In another row sat Helen Langhanke, the plain-looking woman who had delivered the divinely favored defendant into the world. In fact, she had never enjoyed that miracle. As Mary would discover when her mother died and left behind her own diary, Helen hated her daughter.

Mary and Woolley took seats at the long table assigned to them. Woolley, even in July, wore a dark gray suit. He meant business no matter what the season. The attorney and his client carefully avoided eye contact with Thorpe and his lawyer at the other end of the table as they awaited the arrival of Judge Goodwin Knight. Although only forty, he was already white-haired. His always smiling, avuncular face disguised large political ambitions. Mary fidgeted and looked nervous. Smoking was not permitted.

The judge arrived. Thorpe's lawyer, Joseph Anderson, called his client as his first witness. Had the doctor ever entertained women overnight in his home? Thorpe emphatically denied it. Whereas he did observe that when he drove to Mary Astor's home once to pick up his daughter, he found his ex-wife hopelessly inebriated. Then came Woolley's cross-examination:

> *Dr. Thorpe, do you recognize this card I have in my hand?*
> Uh, it looks like a valentine.
> *And do you see underneath the printed words a hand-written note?*
> Uh, yes . . .

Read it, please.

"How deeply do I love you sweetheart."

And by whom is it signed?

It looks like "Lillian."

Is not Lillian one and the same person as Lillian Lawton Miles, a widow who once worked as your office nurse when you practiced medicine in Tampa, Florida?

Yes, I guess so.

No need to guess, Dr. Thorpe. Facts are facts. Did you not have an intimate romantic relationship with Miss Miles in Florida?

Certainly not—

Dr. Thorpe, were you not in fact married to this same Lillian Lawton Miles?!

That is utterly untrue and false.

[Anderson] *Objection! Irrelevant!*

[Woolley] *Your honor, the plaintiff will prove that when Franklyn Thorpe married my client Mary Astor, he and Lillian Lawton Miles were still man and wife!!—and that he tricked her into a bigamous marriage.*

The ensuing hubbub may have given Mary a flashback to the courtroom scene of *The Case of the Howling Dog*, a 1934 Perry Mason mystery for Warner's that also involved a diary—surely here the part would call for more than just screaming attractively. Knight gaveled the buzz into silence.

Woolley's next witness was Nellie Richardson, Marylyn's English nanny, already a common Hollywood affectation of the time. She testified that Thorpe had "at least four different women" stay over-night. One of them was Norma Taylor, "a rather flashy blonde." (Miss Taylor's movie career had ended a year earlier after her small part in Republic Studio's *Tumbling Tumbleweeds*.)

> *Do you remember anything unusual about her?*
> Well, one night I was in the dining room eating with little Marylyn, and she staggered in looking angry. I think she was tipsy.
> *What did you do?*
> Well, I was scared. She picked up a brass candlestick and was about to throw it into the mirror when Dr. Thorpe rushed in and grabbed her.

Nellie said Thorpe had called the police.

Officer Walker of the LAPD, next up, confirmed her account. He had come upon Thorpe and Norma grappling on the bathroom floor, and he and his partner ejected her from the premises. Thorpe had shown him wounds where Norma had stabbed him twice in the leg with a carving fork.

After Walker's appearance, Woolley introduced statements from various Floridians who believed Lillian Miles and Thorpe were man and wife. Mrs. Miles was present in the courtroom. "Dr. Thorpe and I are only good friends," she told reporters. She said she would sue someone for a blackened reputation.

The next day's tabloids carried Lillian's picture on their front pages. Norma Taylor appeared as well, dubbed "The Blonde Fury" in the New York *Daily Mirror*. To restore her self-esteem she fled

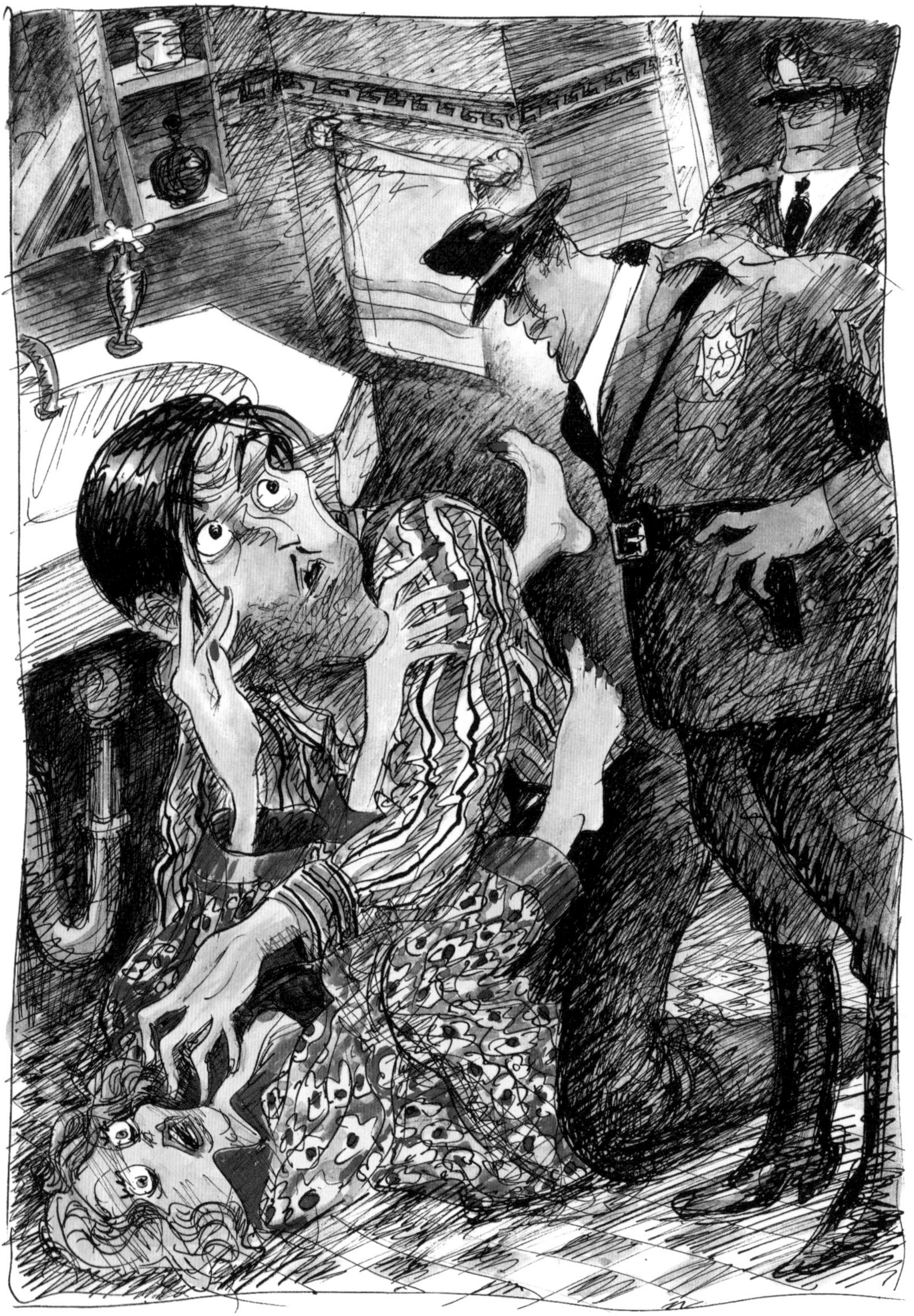

Hollywood the next day for the insulating arms of the asbestos heir and legendary playboy Tommy Manville, then only married to wife No. 3 of an eventual eight, all blondes.

Mary made her much-anticipated debut on the witness stand on Thursday evening. Woolley sympathetically led her through an account of Thorpe's failings as a father. "He was a harsh disciplinarian," she testified, wringing her handkerchief. "He shook [Marylyn] so hard her teeth rattled and cut her lips. Then he'd spank her and there would be bruise marks on her little body." Mary sobbed controllably—just as she had in *Dinky* (1935), playing a mother framed and sent to prison, while Dinky, in military school, wonders why Mommy never visits.

Friday night, with Mary again on the stand, Anderson asked the actress whether the *G* in her diary was "not in fact Geor——" Woolley jumped up to object but was overruled by Knight. Now Thorpe's attorney promised the court that the defense would go "very thoroughly into the unfitness of Miss Astor to have the child's custody. We can prove *in her own handwriting* that she willfully abandoned the child for a married man—*George S. Kaufman!!*" Knight again pounded for quiet.

Kaufman's name added a welcome touch of Broadway elegance to this tawdry exhibition of Hollywood Babylon excess. And the playwright himself was actually in Los Angeles. Anderson demanded he be subpoenaed as a witness; Knight agreed.

As Friday's session ended, Thorpe felt like a poker player who had an ace for his down card. Monday he would have the pleasure of seeing Kaufman mortified on the witness stand, and tomorrow the tabs would print his leaked diary excerpts. These were entries

Florabel Muir had not seen because they were forgeries, perhaps by Thorpe. They praised G's prowess as a lover in such graphic terms that even the tabloids resorted to euphemisms. The most explicit extracts appeared in *Time*, which quoted Mary's testimonial to her "thrilling ecstasy" with George, who "fits me perfectly . . . many exquisite moments . . . twenty—count them, diary, twenty . . . I don't see how he does it . . . he's perfect."

Even before Judge Knight ended Friday's session, some reporters sneaked out of the courtroom in an attempt to find Kaufman before others did. He was known to be staying at the Garden of Allah, a kind of bed-and-brothel favored by writers from New York because of the discretion of its staff, the privacy of its bungalows, and the wildness of its parties. Kaufman was not much for those, but he did enjoy the company of the starlets who decorated the swimming pool.

Unable to ditch the reporters who pursued him there, George finally opened the door to them and tried to appear relaxed and casual. His distinctive pompadour, looking as wild as the hair on the bride of Frankenstein, seemed to give him away. "I was just a friend of Miss Astor like many others in Hollywood," he said as nonchalantly as he could. "I have attended many of her parties as a guest and friend. I most certainly am not involved in the difficulties with Dr. Thorpe." A decorous bid to duck the exploding scandal.

Instead, the typesetters knocked themselves out emblazoning his name across the Saturday papers. Kaufman panicked. *What would Beatrice do when she heard about all this?* She was touring Europe with Ellin and Irving Berlin. *What would his friends in the theater think?* The toast of Broadway was now badly burned. The poised,

take-command lover Mary described in her diary was also a shy man with a bundle of phobias—scared of microbes, failure, and death.

The prospect of being grilled in court about his intimate affairs terrified this very private man, and he had to get out of California *before the subpoena was served.* Kaufman made a frantic call to MGM's "boy genius" producer chief, Irving Thalberg, to save him from the law. Thalberg, thirty-seven, second in command at MGM, had lured the proud citizen of Broadway back to glitzy Gomorrah the preceding year with an offer of $100,000 to coauthor the Marx Brothers' first film for MGM, *A Night at the Opera*, with Morrie Ryskind. Thalberg was the only movie producer Kaufman respected, and the feeling had become mutual after the playwright—author of a fierce clause in the Dramatists Guild contract, informally named for him—once responded to pressure for a rush treatment with, "Do you want it Wednesday, or do you want it good?"

Thalberg, who had a heart condition and always looked frail, was planning a weekend cruise on his yacht, *Melodie*, with his wife, Norma Shearer, who had recently starred in Irving's worst box office flop, *Romeo and Juliet*, playing—at the age of thirty-four—the doomed teenager. Lillian Hellman once described Shearer as having "a face unclouded by thought." Nevertheless, as long as her husband was head of production at MGM, he would see to it that Norma kept her status as "the first lady of Hollywood." Kaufman, assured by Thalberg that their cruise would take them beyond the three-mile limit, had gratefully accepted an invitation to join them. But the sheriff's men boarded the yacht off Catalina Island. There the officers served their summons on America's newly crowned Great Lover.

Two years earlier, after working for Sam Goldwyn, who had refused to pay him for the screenplay he had written as a vehicle for the popular comedian Eddie Cantor, Kaufman vowed never to return to this hellhole. Now he cursed himself for having broken his promise.

Aside from Goldwyn's stiffing him for work done, Kaufman had always held Hollywood in low regard. He hated spending time there. Once when a gossip columnist for the *Los Angeles Examiner* asked him to give her the names of the guests at a party given at the Trocadero, the fabled nightclub of the 1930s, the playwright created his own list. In addition to the actual guests there—Sylvia

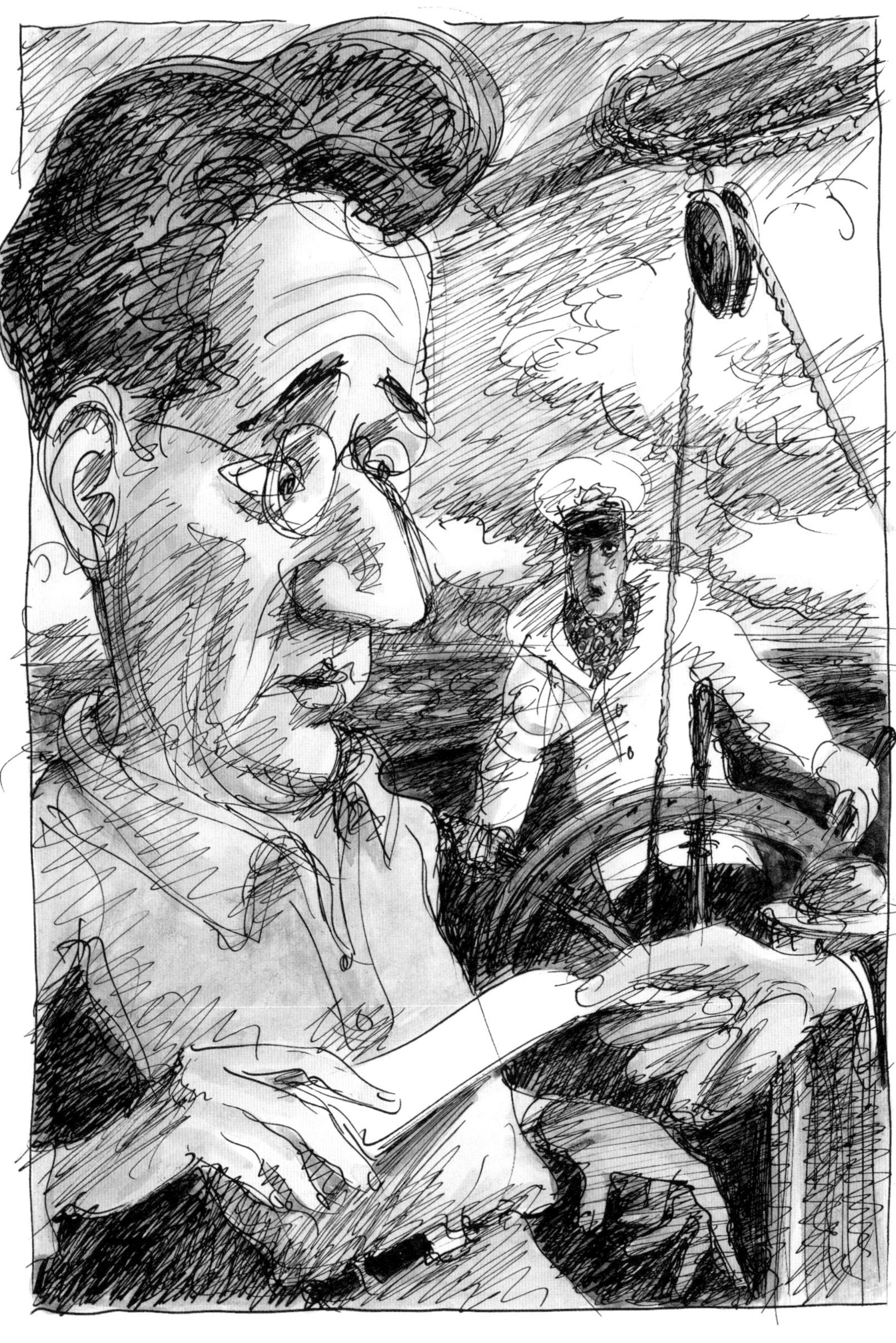

Sidney, Richard Barthelmess, Groucho and Zeppo Marx—George added Karl Marx, William Cullen Bryant, Edith Cavell, and Ethan Frome. The list was printed in full. For all anyone in Hollywood knew, the unfamiliar names were new contract players.

But now Hollywood would pay back the smart-ass with a scandal that would stick to him forever. "Forget it," said Irving and Norma: the feeding frenzy would be over in a few days. George didn't buy it. With newsmen from every paper and every wire service in the USA, much less the world, stalking him, how was he ever going to escape? Moss Hart, the sartorially elegant collaborator with whom he had written some of his greatest hits, had recently moved to nearby Malibu. Surely Mossie could come up with something—all he had to do was pretend they were stuck for a second-act curtain, and Hart would dream up a way to get him out of there.

Wearing a fedora pulled low, the fugitive showed up at Hart's rented mansion, greeting him with a wagging forefinger (no handshakes for George—hygiene, baby). His narrative of the last forty-eight hours had only one bright spot; his lawyer thought the subpoena was "defective." But Judge Knight might think otherwise.

George shared with Hart his fear that publicity from the trial would wound Bea, his smartest critic and indispensable champion. "My God—what if she *leaves* me?" He held his big head and moaned, "After this trial nobody will remember anything I've done—only that I screwed Mary Astor."

Although no one had seen him enter Hart's home, men with cameras were likely to turn up any minute. In his haste he hadn't even brought his trunk. Could someone launder what he had on?

"*Trunk . . . laundry . . .*" A free-associater from his years of psychoanalysis, Hart thought of the Marx Brothers stowing away in a steamer trunk in *A Night at the Opera*, which had just opened six months earlier. He and George brainstormed a plot—yes, life can imitate art—where George would hide in a laundry hamper and be driven to a train. True, a laundry truck on a Sunday might seem odd, but it could work.

Hart figured reporters would stake out the Los Angeles station, so when the truck arrived, the bribed driver was told to take the cargo to San Bernadino. George jackknifed his six-foot frame into the hamper.

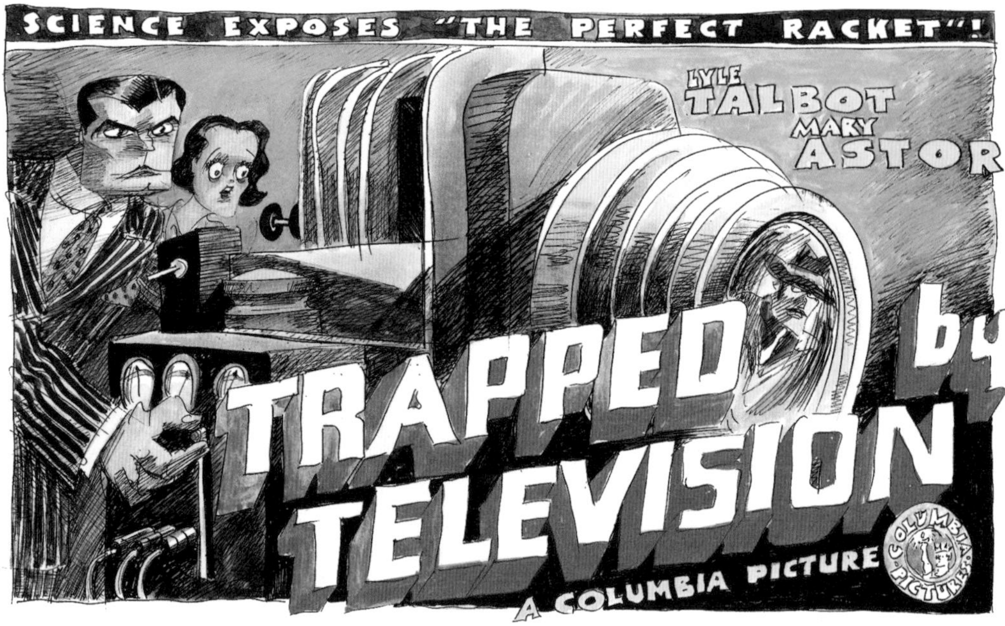
SCIENCE EXPOSES "THE PERFECT RACKET"!
LYLE TALBOT
MARY ASTOR
TRAPPED by TELEVISION
A COLUMBIA PICTURE
COLUMBIA PICTURES

Once at the station, George discovered he had just missed the train to Chicago. With six hours to kill before the next one, he tucked into a nearby movie house. *Trapped by Television* was the second feature, starring Lyle Talbot and—of course—Mary. Television was still confined to laboratories in 1936, but the public was fascinated even by news of the invention.

This was the second movie about the coming phenomenon of "broadcasting moving images." The first, Paramount's *Big Broadcast of 1936*, called the new invention "radiovision" and had an all-star cast headed by W. C. Fields. Columbia's B picture had a no-star cast with Talbot, an actor with almost no forehead, as the brilliant inventor of television. Gangsters kidnap Mary, his girlfriend, to get the idea. There is an obligatory car chase before the lovers kiss, unaware they are being televised.

How Kaufman endured this for two-and-a-half showings I don't know, but when the tabloid's favorite fornicator finally boarded the train, he didn't emerge from his tiny compartment until he reached Chicago, twenty-two hours later—plenty of time to reflect on his wretched situation.

As you know, in all musical comedies the romantic leads must be on the brink of disaster when the first-act curtain comes down. We have reached that point in our story. Our heroine is facing disgrace and complete ruin, and the villain is about to triumph. It is time to ring down the curtain on Act I of the *Purple Diary* and take a ten-minute intermission. I'll use that time to tell you what happened after the unforgivable blunder at my first wedding. Remember the "Farmer in the Dell" episode?

After seven years the marriage fell apart, but it wasn't a total bust. I helped my wife to become an established artist's representative, and she encouraged me to leave my design job at CBS and risk freelancing as an illustrator. Both decisions turned out well. The freelance life suited me, and so did having two healthy, creative, good-natured children around me while I worked. But when the marriage ended suddenly, after a hotel scene right out of a Feydeau farce, I feared losing not only my kids but my profession. I had no savings, and no place to work or live.

But "God tempers his wind to the shorn lamb." Out of nowhere Victor Navasky appeared. Victor in that summer of 1963 was the editor of a struggling humor magazine called *Monocle*. He needed an art director for his monthly periodical, but he had no money, so he offered me a work/space arrangement. I would design and paste up his magazine (this was way before personal computers), and in return I could use his office space to do my own freelance work at night. When I saw that my future office had enough room for me to sleep on the floor, I agreed. Until winter came and the heat was shut off at night, I had a place to stay.

The *Monocle* offices were on what was then the shabby part of Fifth Avenue, below Fourteenth Street. John F. Kennedy was president, and it felt as though the Red Scare of the 1950s had petered out, but magazines were still antsy about satirizing right-wing Cold Warriors. Since that was precisely *Monocle's* purpose, left-wing cartoonists like Tomi Ungerer, Ed Koren, and David Levine, who had just begun caricaturing writers for the *New York Review of Books*, worked for Navasky's page rate of $25 a drawing. Meeting these cartoonists inspired me, and Levine and I became good friends.

At the time I didn't know how to caricature, but when Victor needed a comic portrait I did the best I could. I was heavily influenced by Levine's work—everybody was in the 1960s—but eventually found my own way of doing character assassination. Two years later, when I was offered space for a feature in *Ramparts*, I was ready.

I had started in *Ramparts* in 1966, after Lyndon Johnson (who had actually—few remember—been the peace candidate) had begun sending more and more troops to Vietnam. As protest against the war escalated, magazines that would never before have dreamed of poking fun at the Establishment were now eager for me to do just that. By the time the Vietnamese had won back their country in 1974, my drawings had appeared on the covers of *Ramparts*, the *Nation, Atlantic Monthly, Harper's, Evergreen Review*, the *Village Voice*, the *New York Times Magazine*, the *National Lampoon*, *New York Magazine*, and even *Time* and *Fortune*. I began to feel like a war profiteer. In my defense, I did violate the law by crossing the

Peace Bridge into Canada to deliver medical supplies to the North and South Vietnamese, although I admit it was Nancy's idea. She, our six-month-old daughter, Jenny, several dozen members of the Society of Friends, and I were met by federal agents stationed at the bridge. They said we were breaking the law, but they didn't stop us.

Ah—there's the chime. Intermission is over. I'll tell you about my second marriage later, but now let's get back to our screwball tragedy.

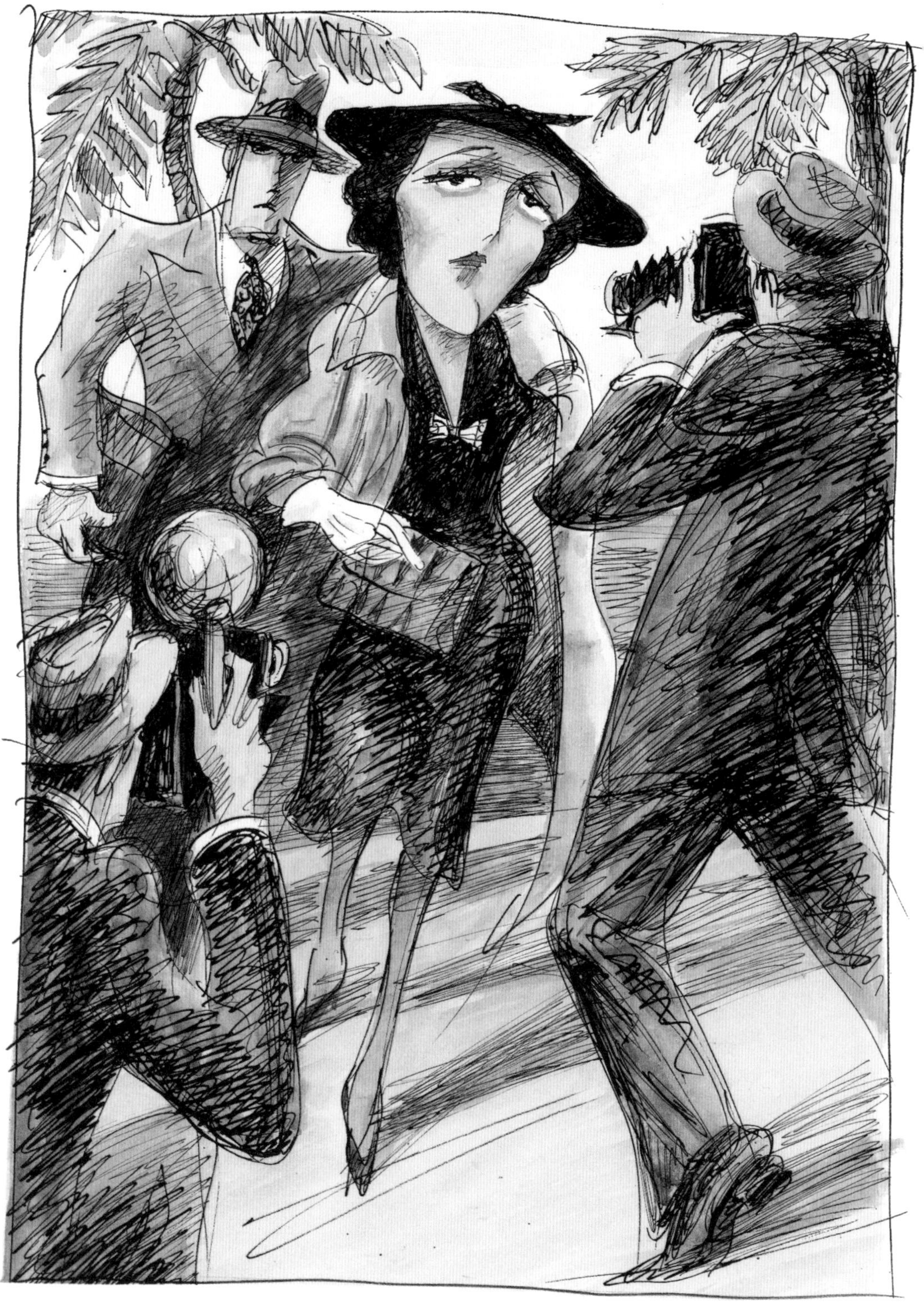

The Trial,
Act II

FTER FRIDAY'S COURT SESSION, where questions were raised about Thorpe's cavorting with drunken women in front of his four-year-old, Judge Knight invited himself to the Astor/Thorpe residence on Saturday evening to determine whether it was a fit environment for little Marylyn. A reporter from the *Examiner*, facing a Sunday paper barren of trial news, had come up with the idea. Knight went for it, smelling a chance for more name recognition. It certainly couldn't hurt his scheme to run for lieutenant governor.

On the night in question Franklyn, Mary, and their respective lawyers, all using their most ingratiating manners, welcomed Judge Knight and the press core to the swank Toluca Lake home. Marylyn must have rather enjoyed being the center of attention—with such busy parents it didn't happen often, and the long-estranged couple pretended this was just how they loved to spend a typical weekend. As Knight posed one last time before examining the accommodating toddler, her parents watched in disbelief as the living room turned into a flashbulb free-fire zone.

It was time to tackle the forensics of custody. "Who do you like better, Mickey Mouse or Minnie Mouse?" he asked the child. "Like 'em both." Who (as a politician, he avoided "whom") did she love more—her "Moms" or her "Pops"? Why, she loved them both! Solomon in his wisdom announced there was no hope for a settlement: "The trial must go on." The curtains stirred with the reporters' sighs of relief.

The court case would resume Monday, then, with Mary due to continue on the witness stand. But what the big wheels in Hollywood were doing behind the scenes that weekend is a story in itself.

First, you have to understand that Governor Frank Merriam had won election with financial aid from the Hollywood studios. They were eager that he defeat the socialist candidate, the author Upton Sinclair, who was running against him on the Democratic line. Merriam assigned Goodwin Knight to this high-profile case to reward him for his fund-raising efforts during that gubernatorial campaign. Given Goodie's ambition to share the ticket with Merriam next time as lieutenant governor, he would do whatever the guv told him to, and the guv in turn would do whatever Louis B. Mayer said, since it was the head of MGM who had been wholly responsible for getting Merriam elected.

In 1934, with the country nowhere near able to climb out of the Great Depression, Upton Sinclair, famous for his muckraking novel *The Jungle* and his socialistic solutions for the ailing economy, had swept the Democratic primary for governor of California. (He was hardly alone in turning to socialism at such a dire time.) Mayer, fearful Sinclair would tax the movie studios to pay for his socialist programs, warned that MGM and other studios would move back east if Sinclair won—not anything he was prepared to let happen. Calling in Irving Thalberg, head of production, Mayer told him to create a fake newsreel showing the disasters that would follow such an election outcome.

Movie theaters were forced to show the film when they booked an MGM movie, and William Randolph Hearst would see to its distribution to all other theaters in the state. And indeed, as soon as the fake exposé hit the screens, Sinclair's huge lead vanished, and Frank Merriam became governor. The dirty politics and stealth tactics of Richard Nixon? As you can see, just a rerun.

With Mary's custody suit about to bring disgrace upon Hollywood, Louis B. decided it was time to call in some IOUs from Merriam. Odds are he phoned the governor to explain how important it was that the diary never surface at the trial—the public must never get a load of the contents. Why, if moviegoers learned what their sainted stars were up to, they might well stay home and listen to the goddamn radio. *Millions would be lost!* It's entirely possible that the governor in turn phoned Knight with Mayer's concerns, but even if he did, as I suspect, on what possible grounds could the judge keep the diary sealed?

Another big wheel careening into action was jug-eared Will Hays, the man the studio bosses chose in 1921 to be in charge of the industry's morals. The Hays Office decided what could be said and shown on screen. His decisions, codified in the Production Code, forbade even the utterance of "damn" (already familiar even

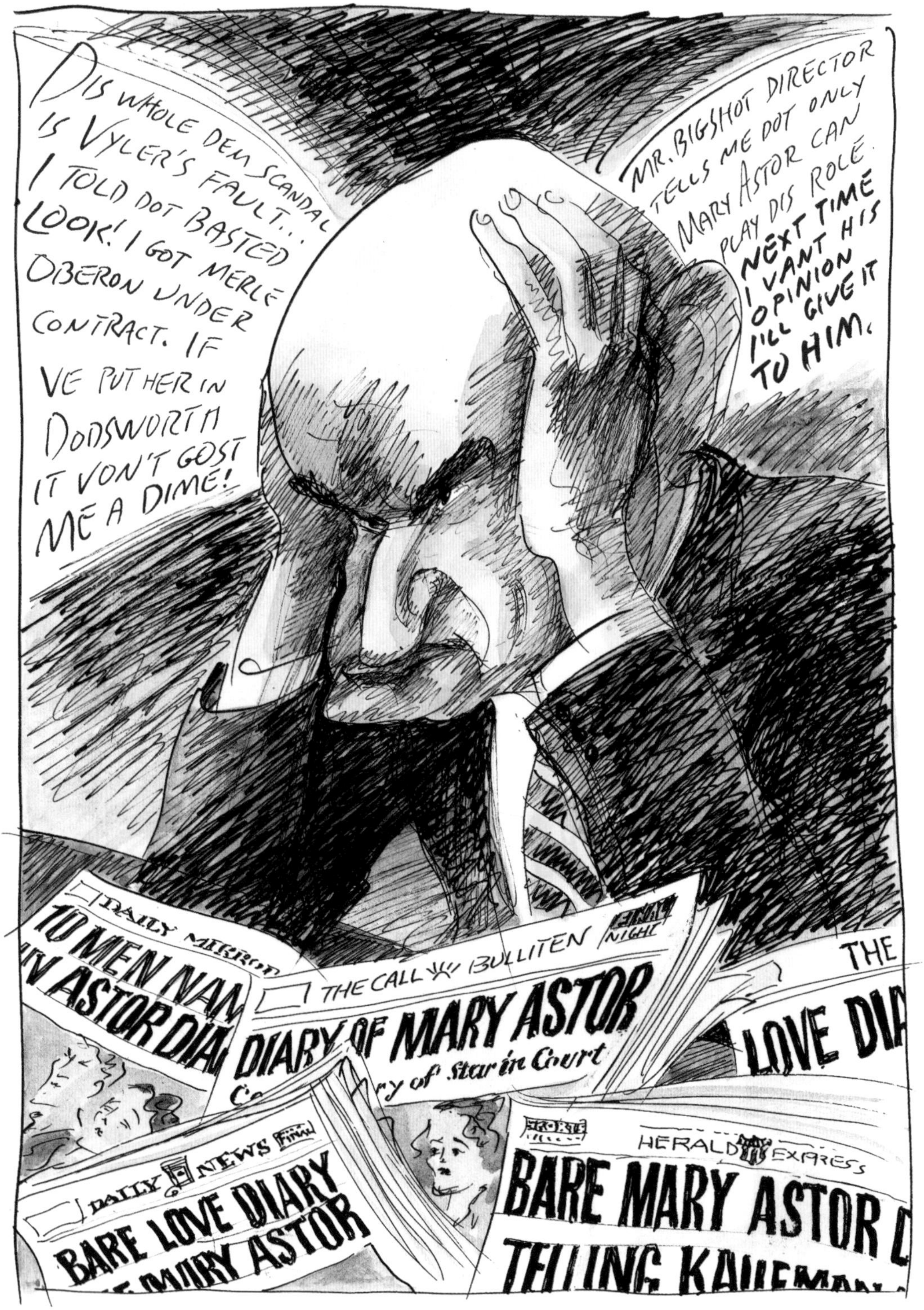
DIS WHOLE DEM SCANDAL IS VYLER'S FAULT... I TOLD DOT BASTED LOOK! I GOT MERLE OBERON UNDER CONTRACT. IF VE PUT HER IN DODSWORTH IT VON'T GOST ME A DIME!
MR. BIGSHOT DIRECTOR TELLS ME DOT ONLY MARY ASTOR CAN PLAY DIS ROLE. NEXT TIME I VANT HIS OPINION I'LL GIVE IT TO HIM.
DAILY MIRROR
TO MEN NAM
N ASTOR DIAR
THE CALL BULLITEN
NIGHT
DIARY OF MARY ASTOR
ry of Star in Court
THE
LOVE DIA
DAILY NEWS FINAL
BARE LOVE DIARY
BARE MARY ASTOR
HERALD EXPRESS
BARE MARY ASTOR D
TELLING KAUFMAN

in silent movies). His chief qualification for the job was his success in having secured the 1920 Republican presidential nomination for the "America First" candidate, Warren G. Harding, a feat made possible in part by an assist from Albert Lasker, the father of modern advertising and the man later responsible for a Kotex branding campaign in which millions of young schoolgirls were lectured on feminine hygiene. With such a mentor, Hays was a solid candidate to clean up Hollywood.

Even though the trial was only two days old, the press was already calling it "the worst case of dynamite in Hollywood history"— and the previous record holder, the Fatty Arbuckle affair of 1921, was thought to have involved rape and murder. (That was the scandal that got the producers to hire Hays in the first place.) While the Movie Czar wanted to lead the charge, he was laid up with a cold; his office enforcer, Joe Breen, was left to carry out Hays's orders. The Catholic Breen believed "profit-hungry-Jews"—always one word to Breen—were to blame for all the schmutz on the screen. These two watchdogs, together with the Catholic Legion of Decency, which threatened a boycott of any Mary Astor movie if the diary became public, posed a real threat to Goldwyn's unfinished film.

On Sunday, Hays stopped hawking phlegm long enough to phone Mendel Silberberg, the general counsel for the Motion Picture Producers and Distributors of America. Silberberg was a "fixer," a lawyer who settled conflicts behind the scenes—quietly, at the highest level. Hays told him to contact the opposing lawyers and Judge Knight and knock their heads together until they settled, and maybe find a reason to delay the trial. Then Hays sent an unofficial announcement to all studio executives, ordering all

actors, publicists, and producers not to comment on the case. A fog of silence settled over Hollywood, even more impenetrable than the fogs used to cover up cheap sets at Universal. When the press called screen stars noted for mouthing off, they had no views at all on Astor. Hays may have been a homely Hoosier with bucked teeth, but it was suicide to ignore him.

As if the custody suit did not have enough headline-making names, another was added on Monday. Mary had admitted that John Barrymore had visited her at home; Thorpe's lawyer now subpoenaed him. The actor was in a sanatorium drying out yet again, and when the court-appointed heart specialist filed his report on the fifty-four-year-old, it stated that he could not now appear in court without endangering his life, and that "unless the screen star coop-erates closely with his doctors he might never be able to appear."

On Monday evening Woolley and his exhausted client, who had rushed to the courthouse from the *Dodsworth* set, entered the large courtroom and noticed that in addition to the overflow reporters in the jury box, more benches had been roped off for out-of-towners brandishing press credentials.

Surprising developments sprang up almost immediately. Where exactly *was* Miss Astor's 200-page diary? Woolley demanded the court be told where the unleaked pages of the book were. Dr. Thorpe was put on the stand and said he'd given the incendiary reading matter to his lawyers. Then Ethel Pepin, who had been on Thorpe's legal team until she protested some of his tactics, swore she gave it to Joseph Anderson. Joe said he had given it to William, his brother and law partner, and Bill said he had had photostatic copies made of pages pertinent to the custody action but didn't know where the rest were.

Since the diary had been tampered with, the court held that the whole thing must be disallowed, and Judge Knight promised that anyone named in it who was not involved in the custody action would be protected.

Another surprise was Mary's assertion during cross-examina-tion by Anderson that Thorpe had been aware of her adultery with Kaufman. She claimed to have told him, "You know George Kaufman has nothing to do with this divorce. You've known about Kaufman since last September [1934], and you've condoned it. Now you bring it up in order to threaten me and obtain custody of my baby."

"Is it not a fact," Anderson persisted, "that you let this divorce go by default because you were in love with George Kaufman?"

"It is not a fact," Mary tartly replied.

"On or about February 8th, 1935, didn't you come to some conclusion about your rights and privileges?" he asked.

"I considered it my right to be free from the brutality of the man, and his constant association with Lillian Miles."

Mary's suit now alleged that Thorpe was not divorced from

Lillian when he married her. And when Anderson kept bringing Kaufman's name into the trial, Woolley objected, declaring that the questions were designed to "scandalize"—"speak falsely of," in legal parlance—"someone not involved in this hearing" and to inject "scurrilous matter to try to injure Miss Astor and indirectly her child."

The objection was overruled, but Knight sustained a later one when Anderson asked, "Were you in love with George S. Kaufman when the divorce was granted?" Mary was not obliged to answer.

Then came the most surprising development: Knight declared an adjournment of the trial for one week, to allow Mary to complete her work on *Dodsworth*. She had begun to show up on the set looking haggard, with dark circles ringing her eyes from the night sessions, and a lawyer for Goldwyn told the court that five hundred people would be out of work if production had to stop because one of its leads could not perform. Whether it was this populist pitch or pressure from Silberberg that got the trial postponed depends on whether or not you share my faith in what was the rock-ribbed sliminess of the studio system.

On Tuesday the resilient actress was back on the Goldwyn set, where Wyler, the director known for being meticulous and picky, had nothing but praise for Mary's interpretation of the urbane widow, Edith Cortright. But late in the day a sad-faced Sam Goldwyn, not yet fully recovered from gall bladder surgery, told her she had to attend a meeting in his office at seven o'clock. Even Wyler did not know why.

When Mary was shown into the conference room along with

Woolley, they were taken aback to see producers from all the major studios, together with their battery of lawyers. Present were A. H. Giannini, who owned not only the Bank of America but also United Artists, where Goldwyn produced his pictures; Louis B. Mayer, a frequent user of the casting couch yet an evangelist for wholesomeness; Irving Thalberg, who did Mayer's dirty work when necessary; Harry Cohn, head of Columbia Pictures, who enjoyed his reputation as a tyrant; Jack Warner, and even Jesse Lasky, who twenty years earlier had transformed Lucile Langhanke into "Mary Astor."

Thalberg rose in all his craven majesty. Speaking for the assembled, he said the plaintiff and her attorney were making a grave mistake. The diary, in addition to creating a scandal devastating to the industry, would probably cause her to lose the case and the child too. They urged her to drop it and seek an out-of-court settlement.

Wolley had gamed out just such a scenario beforehand and Mary did as she'd been scripted. *"I SHALL PROCEED WITH MY CASE AS MY LAWYER HAS ADVISED ME!"* she barked back. In the silence that followed, one of the producers, believed to be Mayer, addressed Goldwyn directly and reminded him that he could exercise the morality clause in Astor's contract and replace her. For once in his life, Sam thought for a moment before he spoke.

"A woman fighting for her child?" he said. "*THIS IS GOOD!!!*"

No bunch of Louis B. Momsers was going to tell Samuel Goldwyn whom to kick out of *his* pictures.

Mary, reassured, returned to the bungalow on the Goldwyn lot where she now lived, hiding from relentless newspapermen who had staked out her home. Waiting for her was Dodsworth him-

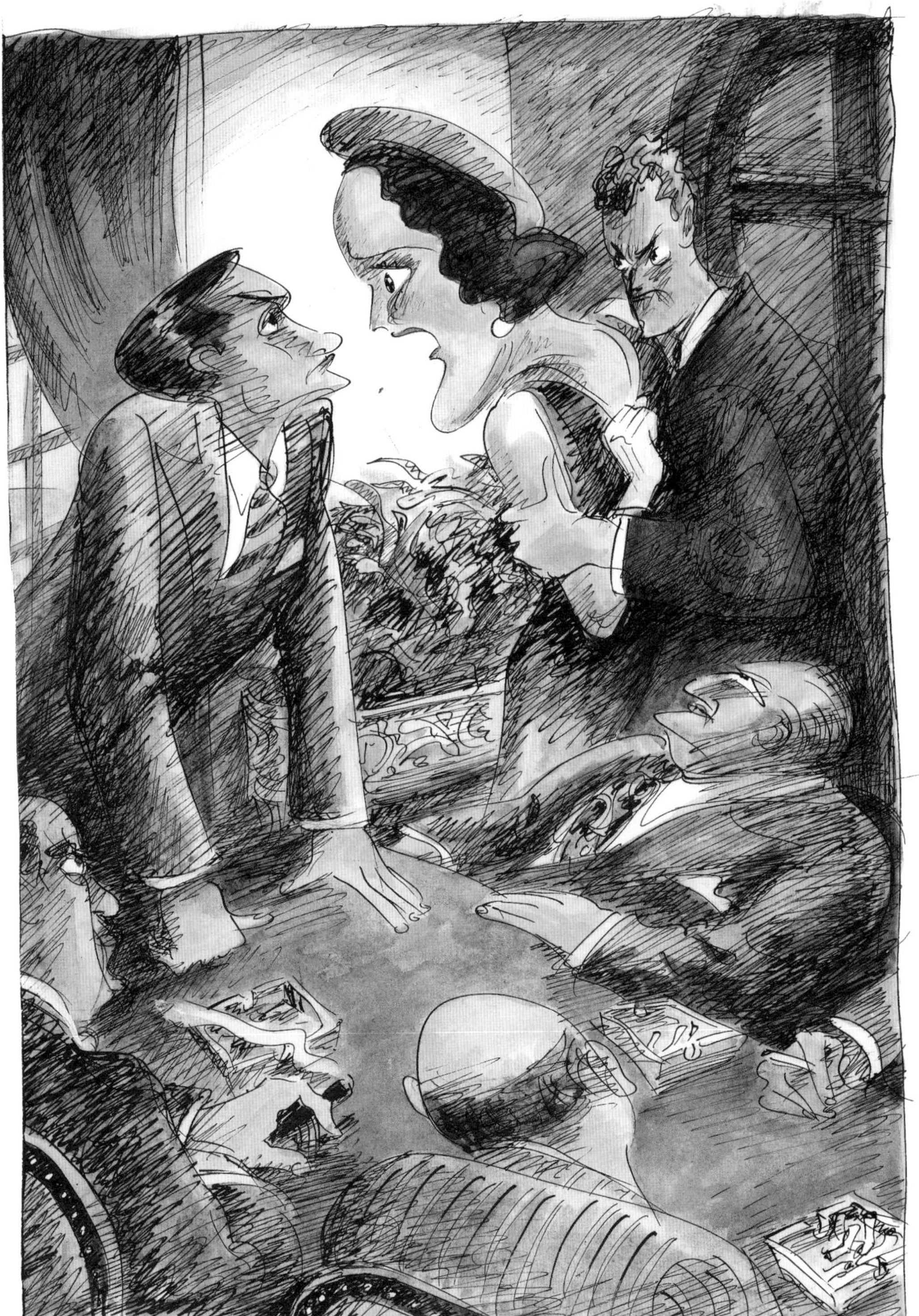

self, avuncular Walter Huston, who had promised to have a bottle of champagne ready to celebrate what he was certain would be Goldwyn's support. On hearing her account of what had just happened, Huston said the one man Sam Goldwyn hated above all others was Mayer, who had forced Sam out after he and Louis had formed MGM. "Once Mayer told him to dump you, your future was secure."

Huston, who had played Sam Dodsworth on Broadway, was perfect for the role of a good-hearted, middle-aged man who runs his own automobile company. For the sake of his wife, Fran, who wants adventure before she grows old, Sam sells his interest in the plant and takes her to Europe. Before long Fran begins to think of herself as a cosmopolitan sophisticate and Sam as dull and provincial. She begins seeing other men and announces that she's leaving him for a minor member of royalty.

Fran is a repellent character, but Wyler wanted her to be "less of a bitch at the outset," lest Dodsworth seem a fool for having married her in the first place. Ruth Chatterton wanted to play Fran as totally self-centered, without any redeeming features. The director insisted it be done his way, all the while smiling, which only increased her outrage. On one occasion she slapped him and stormed off to her dressing room. Thanks to Wyler's intransigence, Chatterton gave her greatest screen performance, but the public held the part against her. *Dodsworth* was the last movie she made in America. After two more movies made in Britain she returned to the stage.

Mary felt the cause of the conflict was Chatterton's hatred of her role, that of a woman "trying to hang on to her youth—which is exactly what Ruth herself was doing."

WYLER WAS NOTORIOUS FOR DEMANDING ENDLESS RETAKES FROM ACTORS, BUT WHEN MARY FINISHES THE FIRST TAKE FOR HER FINAL SCENE, THE DIRECTOR SHOUTS "PRINT IT!"

On the Friday before the Monday that Mary's trial was to resume, Wyler had only one scene left to film. Edith, desolate because Dodsworth has left her to return to his worthless wife, stands on the balcony of her villa in Naples looking out to sea. In the distance is the luxury liner that will take Sam away forever. Then Edith hears the motor of the launch he took out to the ship. And—can it be true?—Sam is in it!! *He hasn't sailed!*

When *Dodsworth* was released, in September 1936, just two months after the trial ended, Mary's performance together with that film's emotional ending would win her forgiveness and new admirers, and mark a turn in her career.

Since I've interrupted the narrative of Mary's life once or twice already, I hope you'll allow just one last intrusion. While Mary is enjoying her triumph in *Dodsworth* seems like a good time to tell you what happened when my first marriage ended.

I was, I assure you, a very shaken man. It seemed to me that I had lost everything. I feared I would lose the love of my two children by not being with them every day; I became depressed and unable to work. With no place to live except the tiny office at *Monocle* magazine, I failed to meet a deadline on an important, high-paying job, and the client took it away from me. The assignment, to caricature dozens of MGM stars, was the kind of job I would normally have looked forward to, but now I just couldn't finish it. I went to a psychotherapist, Dr. Edmund Hilpern. He was a rarity, an old Viennese psychoanalyst who had fled Hitler but wasn't a Jew. We hit it off right away. When I ran out of funds—I was living on borrowed money—he stopped charging me. No kidding.

After one of our sessions he suggested I join him at Sunday

Quaker meeting. I was puzzled. I knew he was a left-winger and assumed he shared my distrust of organized religion. He explained that when the Communist Party in New York had all but closed down in the late 1950s, it urged its departing members to join a church or synagogue to "work for peace." Hilpern joined the Society of Friends, and in the process became a devout Quaker and a disenchanted Commie. The meeting I attended with him was in Earl Hall, a nondenominational gathering place on the Columbia University campus. I had no idea what to expect.

The Friends sat in chairs placed in a circle, and quieted down as eleven o'clock approached. Nothing was said for a long while, and then someone stood and spoke. It may have been about President Kennedy sending "advisers" to Vietnam, and I think it was followed by another comment. What I remember best is the silence. It seemed to charge the room with a connectedness of yearning. After an hour the clerk of the meeting—there is no minister—shook hands with the person on either side of her, and everyone else did the same. Some announcements were made, and then coffee and tea were served.

Since I was the new face in the room, several people introduced themselves to me. Some were "Birthright Friends," and some were "Convinced Friends," meaning members who came from other religions. A surprising number were Jews, which explains the old joke about the rabbi who complained, "Some of my best Jews are Friends."

I became a regular attender and was soon working with the Peace and Action Committee. One Sunday there was a retreat upstate, so there were fewer people at meeting. It was also the first Sunday of the month, when it was the custom to stand at the end of meeting and state your name and describe the kind of work you did. Since

my book *Moon Missing,* a Cold War satire about what happens to international relations when the moon disappears, had just been published, I was able to call myself a writer and illustrator. When the introductions were over, a smiling young woman wearing her hair in a ponytail came with a tray and offered me coffee. She wore no makeup, making it plain that she was radiantly beautiful.

We introduced ourselves and exchanged essential information— she was from Kansas City, Missouri, and was writing entries for the

Columbia Encyclopedia—after which she invited me to her nearby apartment for lunch. I counterproposed that we go to Rumplemeyer's for lunch. I still don't know why I said that. I had never been there, but I knew it was in the Hotel St. Moritz on Central Park South, and was told it had the best hot chocolate. I do recall having enough cash for a taxi with me. The only problem was that neither of us looked as though we belonged in such an elegant setting. She was dressed in a tweedy long skirt and clunky shoes, and I was wearing a corduroy jacket that I had bought the day before in a flea market for fifty cents. (I had my children on Saturdays, and they loved flea markets.)

The maître d' took one look at us and put us in a corner spot where we couldn't be seen. That suited us. We talked. In addition to being beautiful, Nancy had a gentle and soft speaking voice with the clear enunciation that teachers have. She was teaching English as a second language at the United Nations while going for her master's degree at NYU. Her speech was in sharp contrast to my mumbling Bronx accent, which always got worse when I was filled with self-hate, as I was during that period.

I learned Nancy had recently returned from Austria, where she had worked in a displaced persons camp. Eighteen years after the end of World War II there were still hundreds of thousands of refugees without a homeland to go to. Nineteen sixty-two had been declared the Year of the Refugee, when the United Nations determined to settle the homeless. Nancy had decided to volunteer to help.

So she was a goodnik—admirable but worrisome at the same time. What if she was one of those who did good deeds to win favor with God? What if she was *a believer!!*

I don't remember what I asked in order to find out, but she confided that although her Presbyterian parents took her to church regularly, she had rejected the idea of a Supreme Being while she was in college. I, on the other hand, had never "believed," but with my generosity of spirit I was prepared to forgive her early gullibility.

Truth is I fell in love with her the day we met, and as she later would tell me she fell for me that first day as well. She also confessed that when she heard me announce at Sunday meeting that I was a "writer/illustrator" she made sure she was the first one to bring me a cup of coffee. After a week or two I introduced Nancy to my two children, Madeline, seven, and Leo, three. The four of us began attending Quaker meeting on Sundays. Both children loved Nancy, but Leo worshipped her, and would just lie on the floor hugging her legs while she sat in a chair. At Christmas the children and I flew to Kansas City to meet Nancy's parents.

I don't know how Dr. Caldwell and his wife, Ruth, really felt about their daughter's ending up with a left-wing atheist Jew who didn't have a job, much less his own apartment, and was married, no less—but they treated me with every kindness. Two years later, in 1965, after my first wife had obtained a Mexican divorce, Dr. and Mrs. Caldwell drove to New York to be at their daughter's wedding. Their new Chrysler carried an "Honor America" bumper sticker, while my beat-up Studebaker, parked in back of theirs, carried a "Get Out of Vietnam" sticker, but Dr. Caldwell and I pretended not to notice. The wedding was to take place in the same room at Earl Hall where Nancy and I had met.

I wanted very much for my grandmother Pauline Kleinberg, who had come from a shtetl in Romania, to attend my wedding.

Grandma had brought me up while my mother worked in a factory, and when I was eight it was in her tiny apartment that an oxygen tent was set up to keep me alive when I had pneumonia and pleurisy. (It was during my long recuperation that I became an artist, drawing on anything I could get my hands on, usually cardboard that came with the shirts from the Chinese laundry.) Grandma could see how sweet and good Nancy was, but as an Orthodox Jew she couldn't bear the thought of stepping into a church. I assured her there would be no crosses, crucifixes, or statues of saints at Earl Hall, and she came.

The wedding took place after the regular Quaker meeting, and I like to think both my family and Nancy's were moved just a little by the silence. Most of the congregation had stayed on after worship. Also present were Madeline, in a white dress, and Leo, in a sailor suit, a few of my friends, Dr. Hilpern, of course, and our parents—minus my father, whom I didn't want there. After about ten minutes of silence, when the sun suddenly burst through the windows after a rain, Nancy squeezed my hand, and I knew it was time for us to stand and for me to speak my memorized vow: "I, Edward Sorel, take thee, Nancy Lee Caldwell, to be my wife, and promise to be, with divine assistance, a true and loving husband." Then Nancy recited her vows. We sat down again, and those who wanted to speak did so.

Afterward everyone signed a large wedding scroll that a Quaker calligrapher had written, and we went to Butler Hall, overlooking Morningside Park, for wine and wedding cake. There was no band, no "Farmer in the Dell," just the hopes of everyone that it would be a happy marriage. Those hopes were fulfilled.

The Trial,
Act III

WHILE THE CUSTODY TRIAL was in recess, in that summer of 1936, other world events were permitted space on the front pages of the dailies. Franco's rebel forces were closing in on Madrid. Temperatures in New York City reached what is still a record 106 degrees. The Olympics were on in Nazi Germany.

Closer to home, that was the summer when I got separated from my family at Coney Island and ended up in the police station where parents picked up their lost children. I remember not being frightened, which surprised me.

What did scare the family was when a chain of dry-cleaning shops called Spotless opened up a store a block away from my grandfather's shop in the East Bronx. This caused a lot of worry. We knew there wasn't enough business in that poor neighborhood to support two such stores. Spotless's prices were lower than my grandfather's, and if his customers left him to save ten or twenty cents for cleaning a suit he'd lose his shop. This was a time when my grandmother would bargain with a pushcart peddler to charge seven cents for a pound of string beans instead of nine. So saving a dime in 1936 was no small matter—it represented two subway rides.

But the Jews in the neighborhood stayed loyal to my grandfather Hyman Kleinberg. What kind of a name is Spotless anyway? Sounds goyish. That Spotless store closed in less than a year. I remember the night Grandpa came home with the news. He was beaming. He had triumphed over Big Business.

World events, it turned out, did not sell as many papers as Hollywood scandals (when do they ever?), so the tabloids began finding ways to get the scandal back on page one while the trial was in recess. This sometimes meant resorting to unfounded rumors. On August 8 the New York *Daily Mirror*'s front page blared, **$100,000 TO HUSH DIARY**, claiming the producers were willing to pay Mary that much to drop the case. Not so. The next day's scoop, that the Legion of Decency was going to blacklist any actor named in Mary's diary, was for real.

To keep the pot boiling, the *Mirror* got a popular psychologist, Dr. William Marston, to make "a close study of the photographs of the petite film star." As the inventor of the lie detector test and eventual creator of *Wonder Woman*, Marston obviously had the probity for the job. He determined that Mary was "a pleasure seeker, secretive . . . a square shooter . . . an introspective, pugnacious individual," who was "inclined to be oblivious to the ordinary conventions and social rules when she is set on a course of her own." A photo of her face in profile showed that her forehead, nose, and chin barely protruded to the vertical line they had superimposed on the picture. This meant they were "hidden" features, evidence that Mary was a secretive type.

Some papers hired graphologists to analyze Mary's character on the basis of photos of her handwriting from the diary. Another psychologist, Dr. Frank Payne, said only, "Writers of intimate diaries are victims of infantile exhibitionism."

Dr. Thorpe expressed a similar notion in "I Married an Actress," his newly syndicated feature in the *Daily News*. His photo ran with the series, but there was something about his Clark Gable mustache that made him appear, I thought in hindsight, less like a hero and more like a villain. "The trouble with Miss Astor," he wrote, "—the trouble with many like her in the movie industry—is that they think they are royal aristocrats, answerable to no one for their actions." He went on to describe his shallow ex-wife as loving "idle gossip, chatter, parties, and social gaieties." Then why did the sensitive lover of the outdoors marry her? He was "lured" into it as a result of intimacies she *forced on him* while he was treating her. But he could not bring himself to say he was sorry he had married her. "For, over and against the sorrow, the bitterness, the disappointments that have shadowed my life, one ray of bright sunshine shines," he wrote: "Little Marylyn, my daughter."

Newsmen went after any man named in the diary. No stud was left unturned. The press even dug up Bennett Cerf, who had barely been mentioned. He laughed when told in what context his name appeared. "Well, well! So she broke that date with me to go out with George, did she? In the light of everything that's happened since, it would appear a broken date made that one of the luckiest days of my life." Lest anyone think he'd fallen on the wrong side of Mary's love ledger, he added, "Our meetings were always casual, and we were never alone."

In London, a besieged Beatrice Kaufman was finally forced to meet with reporters. She dismissed George's affair as a harmless flirtation and refused to play the wounded party. "George is a good husband. I love him very much, and he is in love with me. Please do not ask me to discuss Miss Astor. She is a film actress who kept a diary. Very stupid, that." It wasn't headline material, but it was a chance to run through the scandal again and publish an unflattering photograph of the publicly shamed wife, for whom travel had been too broadening.

In Los Angeles and New York, wags short of material had taken to turning up their coat collars, pulling their hats over their eyes and furtively whispering to the crowd, "I have to leave town. I just found out I'm in the diary." The very word "diary" had become risqué, so that every fan magazine tried to capitalize on it. The October issue of Fawcett's *Movie Classic*, for instance: EXCLUSIVE! FRED MACMURRAY'S HONEYMOON DIARY. MacMurray, now best remembered as the scheming insurance agent in *Double Indemnity* (1944), was in 1936 an up-and-coming leading man, a heart throb for young women after he appeared with Katharine Hepburn in *Alice Adams* (1935).

George Kaufman, who was still in hiding, was blindsided by some of the diary passages he read. He asked that Moss Hart in California be permitted to secretly examine the diary—the only friend he would trust on such a mission. Moss reported back that the actress had indeed written the phrase "twenty—count them, diary, twenty," but that it referred not to his sexual performance but to his string of Broadway hits.

Monday, August 10, the trial resumed, and it started with the issuing of a bench warrant for the arrest of George Kaufman for failing to show up as ordered. Thorpe's attorney reported that he had phoned Irving Thalberg, who said George had "disappeared." Judge Knight warned that should Kaufman ever return to California he would be subject to prison. "The law is no respecter of persons, be they prominent, rich, intelligent, dumb or stupid." Oliver Wendell Holmes he wasn't, but Knight did run a pretty tight courtroom.

As soon as Mary was seated in the witness box, she underwent intense grilling about her "friendship" with the men named in her diary: John Barrymore, the screenwriter George Oppenheimer, Cerf, Daniel Silberberg (a New York stockbroker), and Kaufman. Although Anderson's cross-examination was fierce and unrelenting, Mary handled it splendidly, with far more composure than she had a week before.

The secret of her newfound self-assurance was her decision to go on pretending she *was* Edith Cortright, her character in *Dodsworth*. "She was a lot of things I wasn't, she was a lot of things I would like to have been," she said in her 1959 memoir. "She had also been a little foolish and human. But she had complete confidence in herself, and I had very little. She was not talkative. She listened to everyone with a gentle No-comment smile. She walked tall; she made no unnecessary gestures, or movements. She was *cool.*"

And from all reports, that's just how Mary was in the witness box. She sat a little straighter, kept her white-gloved hands quiet, and took a long time before answering questions, which unsettled Anderson. She was never "smart" or "clever," but thanks to playing Edith, she was "rattleproof."

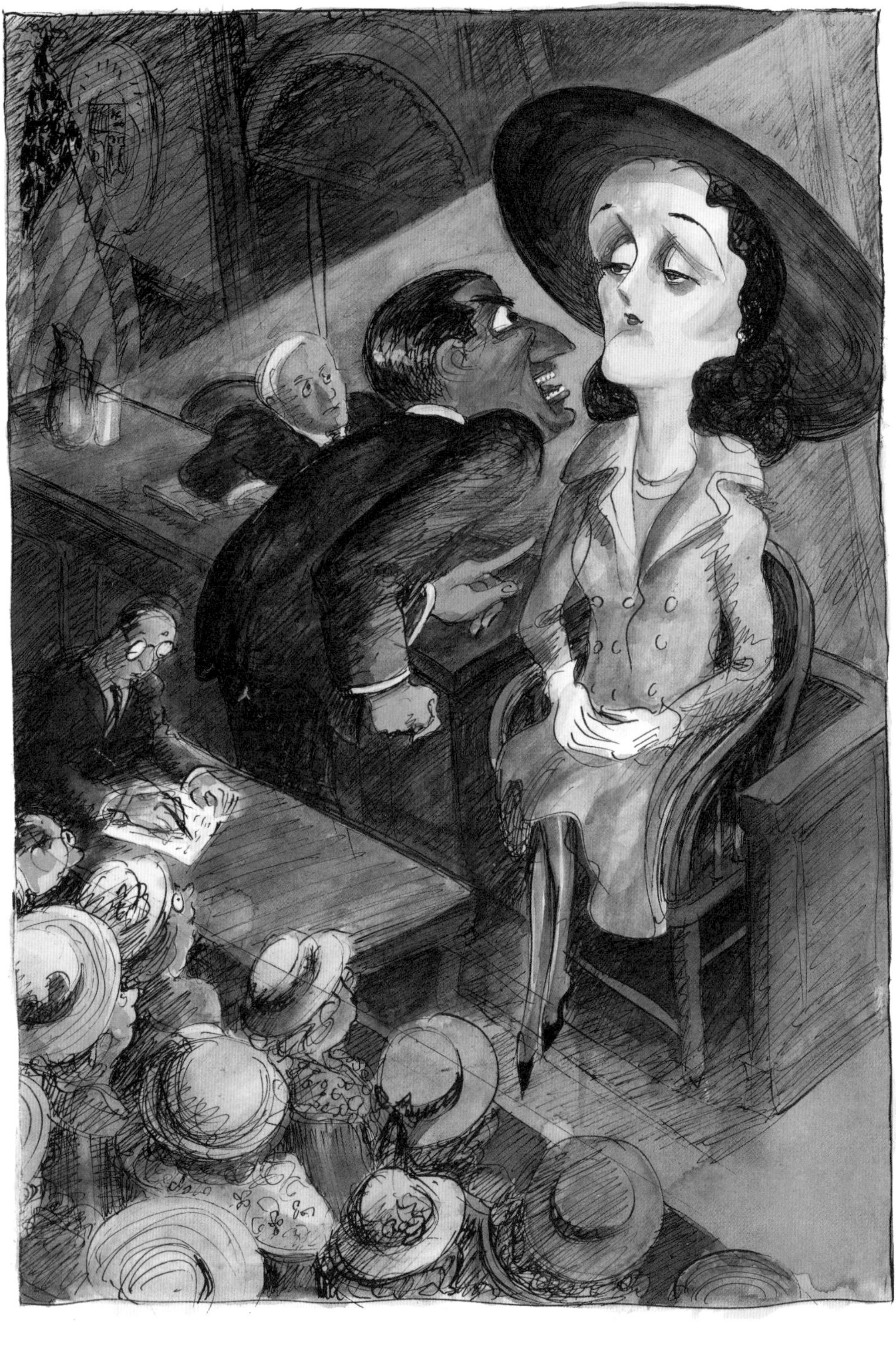

Anderson asked Mary about visits from Oppenheimer, and a mysterious Count Alfonso Carpegna. She did not, she insisted, have drinks served to herself and Oppenheimer in her bedroom, or to the count. Nor had she ever returned to her home under the influence. Then Anderson brought up Barrymore's visit, describing the actor as so intoxicated that he fell over Marylyn while giving details of his latest trip across the country. The lawyer claimed the little girl had had to be rescued.

Mary conceded that Barrymore had called on her in the child's presence and discussed his troubles, but denied he was drunk or had fallen. Judge Knight decided there had been "no particular menace to the child." Anderson dropped the subject but added, "We shall hear more of Barrymore later—*much more.*" But since there was no way to get a very sick Barrymore into court, nothing more was heard.

Jack's liver was not the only thing ailing him. An infatuated twenty-one-year-old actress named Elaine Jacobs, who changed her name to Barrie so it would be closer to his, had recently pursued him from New York, and the couple the press dubbed "Ariel and Caliban" was often the occasion for risible coverage of their public brawls, separations, and reconciliations. They married in Yuma, the charmed site of Mary and Franklyn's own nuptials. Elaine later complained that Barrymore's biographer had depicted her "as a combination of Lilith and the inventor of diphtheria."

Thorpe's lawyer was eager to disprove Mary's contention, made during the previous session, that her husband had overlooked her affair with Kaufman. Here's a smidgen of the cross-examination that followed, giving a sense of Mary's command.

Q.—At the time you had this conversation with Dr. Thorpe, when you said he had condoned your action with George Kaufman, was anything said as to what conduct you had had with George Kaufman?

A.—No, inasmuch as it had no bearing on the issue. He probably mentioned it—that he could use it against me.

Q.—Don't you recall Dr. Thorpe telling you that you had been living with George Kaufman in various places in the United States?

A.—No, because that is not true.

Q.—Didn't he tell you that you had been living with George Kaufman in Palm Springs?

A.—No, he didn't and that is untrue.

Q.—Well didn't he tell you that you had been seeing George Kaufman at the Beverly Wilshire Hotel?

A.—Yes, because I told him so.

Mary said she told her husband that her relationship with Kaufman had nothing to do with the divorce she wanted, but that he "said he intended to use it to get what he wanted."

In answer to another question about their home life, Mary said Franklyn had scolded their daughter nearly every time he came home, and always "in a fit of vile, maniacal temper." Reprising what she had told Woolley, she said Thorpe "would take hold of her and jerk her and spank her roughly. I can't fix the last time—it happened too often." Mary testified that upon returning from her visit to see Kaufman in Palm Springs, she had found several bruises on her daughter's body the size of Thorpe's hand. And prior to the divorce, she said he had "allowed Marylyn to be present while we were quarrelling, while he was threatening me, shaking his fist at me and pushing me into the chairs." She had implored Franklyn to take Marylyn out of the room while they argued, but he said, "No, let her sit there. She's got to learn to sit still."

When I read this part of the trial transcript, I was shaken. I wasn't shocked by Thorpe's fury, which was to be expected from a cuckolded husband, or by his unconcern with the pain he was causing Marylyn, but I was appalled at Mary's inability to protect her daughter from that hate-filled scene. Where was the ferocity she would show with Peter Lorre in *Falcon*, when she kicks him in the shins? How could she sit silently while her terrified daughter was forced to witness the hatred her parents now had for each other? Why was Mary powerless everywhere except on a movie sound-stage?

Nevertheless, I couldn't help rooting for her as I read the rest of the trial transcript. When Anderson asked, "Isn't it true that you have consumed one-fifth of a gallon of Scotch whiskey a day, since your divorce?" Mary firmly said, "No."

> Q.—On April 5, 1935, didn't you say you were perfectly satisfied with the divorce settlement, at a conference with Dr. Thorpe and his attorneys?
> A.—Yes, because—

The judge banged his gavel, and ordered the property settlement agreement to be produced the next day. Court recessed.

Now, in case you forgot, Mary also had a suit pending to set aside the divorce decree and the property settlement, and to have the marriage annulled on the grounds that Thorpe was already married when they wed. If Mary won *that* suit, she would not only win back her daughter and get back her money from Franklyn, but she would ipso facto again be persona grata with the Catholic Church, since she would no longer be a divorced woman. Although Mary was not born a Catholic, she had begun to believe that the Church was her best bet for salvation.

As I've said, I'm a proselytizing atheist. For a while in the 1970s I had a regular feature in both the *Village Voice* and *Penthouse*, and an occasional one in the *Nation*, that allowed me, now and then, to ridicule organized religion. Among my favorite targets was Cardinal Cooke, who went to Vietnam to tell American troops, "You are friends of Christ by the fact that you came over here." Although most of my attacks were against the Catholic Church, most of the canceled subscriptions the *Nation* got because of my cartoons were from Jews, who were outraged by any criticism of their tribe, but especially by one cartoon where I made Mayor Ed Koch's nose bigger than it was. One letter to the editor compared me to Julius Streicher, the Nazi propagandist.

My friends know I regard *all* religions not only as a threat to world peace but as a threat to anything liberating. They'll be flummoxed to discover that the woman I've been daft about for half a century was *a believer!*

Look, I never said Mary and I were a perfect match. But when you get right down to it, isn't every couple odd? Why would Chopin, who had TB, fall in love with a woman who smoked cigars? Why would Donald Trump, who prides himself on his good taste, fall in love with Donald Trump? I mean, who can explain these things? Obsessions by their very nature defy reason.

Besides, there's something to be said for empathy. Remember Othello explaining why he and Desdemona fell in love? "She loved me for the dangers I had passed, and I loved her that she did pity them." Once I read about Mary's psychologically abusive childhood, I did pity her—I pitied all the dangers she had passed.

Shortly after that day's session ended, Mary's hopes of getting an annulment were dashed. From Tampa, Florida, where Thorpe once lived with Lillian Lawton Miles, came a sworn deposition from a Mr. and Mrs. Robert O'Neal, stating that Mrs. Miles, who was the surgeon's nurse, may have given the impression that she was Thorpe's wife "to keep him out of competition," but that Thorpe had never introduced her as his wife.

Still, Woolley might yet claim it was a common-law marriage, or maybe find a record of their wedding somewhere.

This now was the eleventh hour for Will Hays, Mendel Silberberg, and the moguls of the motion picture industry to keep the case from reaching even more ghastly proportions. Directors, producers, and actors, many of them afraid they were mentioned in the diary, had spent a frantic weekend phoning each other to discuss strategy. It seems almost certain that Judge Knight received many of those calls. By Tuesday, August 11, he had had enough. He ordered the attorneys for both principals to prepare their case "on new lines."

"Meet together if you wish and get down to business if you

can," he instructed. He granted a four-hour postponement until two o'clock. But by two, none of the attorneys had returned to the courtroom, and a stay of another hour was announced. This was preceded by a stern rebuke to Anderson and Woolley: "This case has gone on entirely too long. All these extraneous matters and the mudslinging have no direct bearing on the case."

After two days of wrangling, Thorpe still refused to surrender his rights to future access to the diary in case further legal action was needed to answer Mary's pending suit for an annulment. Meanwhile, reporters had learned that George S. Kaufman was not Miss Astor's last love. George had been supplanted in her affections by one of his best friends, whose name would surely have been disclosed had the hearing gone on.

The scoop appeared on August 12 in the *Daily Mirror*, announcing that the best friend, an unnamed dashing broker and bachelor, maintained a seven-room penthouse on Park Avenue, complete with butler and maid. Kaufman had introduced Mary to "Mr. Big" in December, according to the *Mirror*. Shortly after, he and Mary had fetched up in Havana, and she had visited the penthouse often when Kaufman was not present.

Mary was set to return to the witness box and presumably be prodded all over again when Knight unexpectedly called a halt to the proceedings, again bawling out the attorneys for their malicious attacks and waste of taxpayer money. They were there to determine which parent should have custody of a four-year-old—not reopen the goddamn divorce. He told them to prepare the case so the matter could be cleaned up in three days, max.

And lo, it came to pass. The settlement was submitted to Superior Judge Knight at 10 a.m. on August 13, and since he had all but dictated the terms, he approved them. Marylyn was awarded to her mother during the school months, and to her father for vacation periods and weekends. The child's teachers, governesses, and nurses would be selected by mutual consent and the costs shared.

As for the diary, its final disposition rested with the court. "It is part of the agreement," said Thorpe's attorney, "that no one, save the litigants, their counsel and the court, will ever know what became of that diary. It will remain a mystery."

Because the case was settled out of the courtroom, there were no photographs of Mary hugging Marylyn for the front page. Tabloids used what they had in their files. The *Daily Mirror* unaccountably ran a photo from *Red Dust*, showing Mary Astor falling into the arms of Clark Gable beneath the banner,

ASTOR DIARY BATTLE ENDS;
Judge Locks Up Love-Book.

And Then What?

------◇------

WHEN *DODSWORTH* OPENED two months later, there were lines around the block at New York's Rivoli Theatre. Mary snuck into a theater in Los Angeles to catch it. As soon as the audience heard her voice offscreen they burst into applause. She said it was one of the most satisfying moments in her life.

Goldwyn was happy, too, at first. Reviews were excellent, and Huston was nominated for an Oscar. Sinclair Lewis telegraphed, "I do not see how a better picture could have been made." But box office returns soon dwindled. Sam believed that the reason it wasn't a hit was that the leads weren't attractive enough. He planned to do a remake later with Clark Gable (!) as Dodsworth, but by then it was a classic.

Mary moved on to two rousing adventure films, *The Prisoner of Zenda* and *The Hurricane.* Having stirred the affection of the public, she could have made a new start. Instead, she returned to her self-destructive habits, as she admitted in *My Story*: "Sexually I was out of control. I was drinking too much, and I was brought up short when I found myself late in the evening thinking that someone was 'terribly attractive'—and wondering the next morning 'why, *why!*'"

When Mary had no partner she would, as she later wrote, drink, and her loneliness repeatedly led her to believe, after a single springy night in the sack, that she had found her redeemer. Next up would be Manuel Martinez del Campo, a Mexican socialite and polo player raised in England whose father was in the British diplomatic service.

A woman director from London had introduced them, assuring Mary that the handsome twenty-four-year-old was a class act, and not to worry about the seven-year age difference. Both of them hung back, sharing a lunch and a dinner before deciding they were in love. When Manuel's father died suddenly in Mexico City, Mary chartered what AP called "the elopement plane" and flew to Arizona, where they had the Yuma curse laid on them at four in the morning before the groom flew on alone to the funeral (they would stage a proper wedding later). Only afterward did Mary think to ask her daughter whether she liked him. Yes, said Marylyn; "I like potatoes, too."

Del Campo, as became increasingly clear, had no profession—AP referred to him as "an insurance salesman with histrionic leanings"—but he had a Brit accent, and indeed thought it might be nice to do a little acting. Mary set about making his dreams come true, just as she had with Otto and Ken and Franklyn. Between movie assignments she began appearing in stage productions so that "Michael Field" could act too; sadly, he couldn't.

When she was working on a film at Metro, she begged an executive to find him any kind of work. Within a week or two Mike was complaining that "Mary Astor's husband should not have to work as a lowly cutter."

Then he began finding fault with the Toluca Lake home. With the dough Mary was getting from radio and her contract with Columbia, surely they could afford something finer. He found a mansion on San Remo Drive that called for a second servant and tons more furniture. At the Westside Tennis Club he spent days swanning around in his whites, hoping some producer would recognize his potential for stardom. Until then, Mary could pay for a couple to run the house, a full-time gardener, two cars, a stable with a jumper for him and a polo pony for her, membership in the Riviera Country Club, and weekly Sunday brunches for friends, catered by the Brown Derby.

In June 1939, two years into the marriage, Mary gave birth to a son, Tono. Months later, with Britain at war, Manuel enlisted in the Royal Canadian Air Force. Mary was planning for a proper Catholic wedding when he returned—to give the union "a solidity and dignity it had not had"—but in the event he asked for a divorce. This time there would be no custody battle.

In my eagerness to show you the kind of material Mary took to the altar—No. 4 is yet to come—I haven't talked much about her films. Some are worth a few words. *Midnight* (1939) was one of the last of the screwball comedies, with a script by Charles Brackett and Billy Wilder, who had arrived in America in 1933. Claudette Colbert and Don Ameche (*ugh*) played the romantic leads, and Barrymore the millionaire husband of a beautiful but adulterous wife—Mary. Although Barrymore was only fifty-seven, he looked old and unwell, and needed prompt cards to get his lines right.

While waiting to perform, the two ex-lovers sat side by side in their canvas chairs. Mary, remembering the long ago, reached over and touched Jack's hand. He snatched it away—*"Don't!"* Then he forced a laugh, saying his wife was the jealous type.

Or was that it? Mary was pregnant with Tono at the time (the cameraman duly shot her scenes above the waist) and no doubt looked particularly radiant. Whereas Jack was newly stuck with the barnacle Elaine Barrie. By the next year the once-great actor would begin to parody himself as a drunken has-been, both on the screen and on the air. In May 1942 he collapsed while rehearsing Romeo for Rudy Vallee's radio show and died soon thereafter of cirrhosis of everything.

It's true that Jack had caused Mary heartache, but he was the first man—one of the few people ever—who responded as much to her mind as to her beauty, and who tried in good faith to rouse her self-regard. In a profession she served too meekly but with honest intelligence, he taught her early critical lessons in integrity.

Bette Davis, a later mentor, also prodded Mary to dig deeper when acting. In 1940 they were both cast in *The Great Lie*. Davis, at the height of her formidable power at Warner's, asked Mary to help her rewrite the weak script. They did a yeoman job with a preposterous plot and improvised brilliantly before the camera.

The film's chief fascination now is Mary's striking skull-shaped hairdo, which briefly sparked a fad. Also noteworthy is how convincingly she played Tchaikovsky's First Piano Concerto, fooling even the reigning piano virtuoso José Iturbi, who saw that her hands matched the soundtrack perfectly. But the lust that Mary and Bette displayed for a dull, porcine George Brent baffled me when I was eleven and had to sit through it at the Luxor, and still seemed absurd when I saw it again recently. Nevertheless, for her role as a bitchy, ruthless, self-centered artist, Mary won an Oscar for Best Supporting Actress.

In point of fact, Mary didn't really win an Oscar, if by Oscar we mean that familiar gold-plated bronze statuette. What actors in a supporting role were awarded was merely a gold-plated *plaque*. It wasn't until 1944 that supporting actors were given the same statuette that leading players got. Mary's win occurred at the 1942 ceremony, when we were at war and it was decided to tone down the event from a banquet to a dinner, and to ban all formal wear. Owing to the nation's need for metal, the statuettes and plaques were made of painted plaster for the first time. Winners were promised gold-plated bronze versions after the war.

Mary's next film allowed her to give what would become the performance of her life and made her a star, if briefly. *The Maltese Falcon* (1941) was screenwriter John Huston's debut as a director. George Raft, whom Jack Warner wanted as Sam Spade, felt a novice director was a risk and refused the role. Huston was happy to get a young Humphrey Bogart. For the role of Brigid O'Shaughnessy the director wanted Geraldine Fitzgerald, but Warner gave the role to Astor. He had seen her performance earlier that year in *The Great Lie.*

Mary was only thirty-five, but drinking already made her look older. Some *Falcon* fanatics insist she was too old to play Brigid, but few young actresses could have acted a role that ran from Brigid's

breathless, artificial locutions in Spade's office to the coarse gun
moll shouting at Joel Cairo—and then to pitiful hysterics when she
realizes Spade won't "play the sap" for her. We keep trying to figure
out who Brigid really is. She pulls away one mask, only to reveal
another.

Mary saw Brigid as not only a congenital liar but somewhat of
a psychopath, the kind who can't help breathing rapidly. Before
going into a scene, Mary would hyperventilate. "It gave me a heady
feeling, of thinking at cross-purposes," she later said. There isn't a
single scene in the entire movie where what Brigid says is at all close
to what she is thinking. When Sam Spade recognizes that she is

fabricating a story and says, "You're good—you're very good," Astor smiles briefly at the compliment, while at the same time showing that she's terrified she'll be found out.

In fact, Mary's performance as Brigid is as memorable as Marlene Dietrich's Lola in *The Blue Angel*, or Barbara Stanwyck's Phyllis Dietrichson in *Double Indemnity*. Mary sensed even then that her performance in *Falcon* was the high point of her career. Although she was pleased to get an Oscar for *The Great Lie* in 1942, she thought she deserved to have won Best Actress as the costar of *Falcon*. The award

went instead to Joan Fontaine for *Suspicion*, in which that genteel actress gave her usual diffident performance. *The Maltese Falcon* was nominated for Best Picture, but its director, John Huston, didn't get a mention. *Falcon* lost to *How Green Was My Valley*, which also beat out *Citizen Kane. Citizen Kane!!!*

Falcon was, of course, such a huge success that a reunion of the leads was rushed out. In *Across the Pacific*, Bogie single-handedly prevents the Japanese from bombing the Panama Canal as Mary thrills—wartime nonsense, but a hit.

Since all Hollywood tales need endings, I must report that Otto Langhanke died in 1943, and Helen succumbed in 1947. Mrs. Langhanke left behind her own diary, and Mary was shocked to discover how much her mother had despised her. Thinking back to her mother's daily visits to her trial, Mary couldn't help thinking that Helen rather enjoyed watching her daughter get the opprobrium she deserved. Even more stunning was reading her mother's rage at Lucile's selfishness and greed. Helen and, presumably, Otto saw themselves as the exploited parties.

Between the deaths of her parents Mary wedded Thomas Wheelock, a stockbroker and recent weatherman for the Air Force in World War II. Within five years he, too, was broke, Mary had $192.86 in the bank, and they owed over $30,000. It became clear they also couldn't stand each other, but neither of them could afford to move out.

When Mary tried to join the Catholic Church in 1949, a priest, Father O'Dea, asked Tommy to sign a paper affirming the chastity of their relationship. Then O'Dea would submit it to the Chancery Office, explaining that finances and children made divorce untenable. It worked. Mary was accepted into the Church and was able at last to receive the sacraments—the seven outward signs, like confession, of inward grace instituted by Christ. But her drinking continued.

When Mary and Wheelock finally divorced, in 1955, she blamed quarrels over his demands for money, and charged him with mental and physical cruelty, and failure to provide "the common necessaries of life because of idleness, profligacy and dissipation."

Freelancing between fewer and fewer pictures became precarious. In 1944, at age thirty-eight, Mary signed a long-term contract with MGM. The studio put her in a string of Technicolor bonbons in which she was demoted to playing mother to Elizabeth Taylor, Kathryn Grayson, Judy Garland, June Allyson, and Margaret O'Brien, among others. While she may have hated these roles, she was awfully good at them. It's worth noting that only a few years after playing a chronic liar and murderess in *The Maltese Falcon*, she was utterly convincing as the warm, caring mother of four in *Meet Me in St. Louis* (1944). She was touching as well in *Claudia and David* (1946), playing the dying mother of Dorothy McGuire. But her drinking got worse.

One exception to the tiresome scripts Metro threw at her was *Act of Violence* (1947). In this black-and-white thriller, Mary played a cynical, aging prostitute. It was such a departure from playing mothers that she was stimulated into sobriety and the creation of a character unlike any she had played before. But once she returned to those sugar-sweet mother roles, her intake of alcohol reached toxic levels.

A year later, *Little Women* (1948) took a particularly heavy toll on her. She was in debt again, and not well physically or emotionally. As a result everything and everyone in that overproduced film put a strain on her. Young Elizabeth Taylor got engaged to Conrad Hilton Jr. and giggled on the phone while everyone waited on the set. June Allyson, who was assigned the role of sensitive and poetic Jo, chewed gum constantly and irritatingly. Worst of all was Peter Lawford's inability to pronounce the word "porcupine" in take after take; it always came out as "porkypine." The young cast found his endless flubs hilarious. Mary did not.

In 1949, with her children in boarding school, Mary, as she revealed in her autobiography, hit bottom and checked into a sanatorium. Upon her release she sought out Father O'Dea again, but in the years ahead not even he could prevent her three suicide attempts. Twice she took pills, and once she slit her wrists while taking a warm bath. Mary was in the papers again, but this time it wasn't fun to read about.

Desperate to stop her dependence on booze and climb out of her suicidal depression, she joined Alcoholics Anonymous. During her attempt at recovery she turned again to religion, this time toward Father Peter Ciklic, a priest-psychologist at Loyola University in Los Angeles. He tried to make her see the value of what she had accomplished despite her failings. "If you are proud that God loves you, that He has given you great gifts, then you are acknowledging His existence and dependence on Him—and that is humility."

That wisdom made perfect sense to Mary. She perhaps found in God the kind, loving father she had never had, one who loved her in spite of all the foolish things she had done. Some may suspect that Mary, being so close to financial ruin, saw God as an ultimate guarantor, but that's too cynical even for me. In any case, Ciklic suggested she write about her life so she could see for herself that she had indeed accomplished a great deal. When he read what she'd written, he told her to make a book out of it.

In fact, she devoted years to that enterprise. *My Story: An Autobiography*, published by Doubleday, came out in 1959. The book, unusually frank and forthright for its time, became a bestseller. She discovered that she loved writing, and followed the memoir with novels that were well received by critics and the public. In 1971 she published *A Life on Film*, a book about her career that became another bestseller. It should be brought back in a handsome edition with more photographs and better reproductions. The writing is smart and sharp.

In her two memoirs Mary became circumspect when writing about her affair with Kaufman, never divulging more than what the public already knew. George, no surprise, never saw her again after the trial and was touchy about any mention of her name. Franklin Heller, stage manager on many of Kaufman's plays, knew better than to mention the Astor case in the playwright's presence. When Kaufman saw Heller with the first issue of *Life*, the new oversize picture magazine, he asked, "Where did you get it?" "Around the corner at the Hotel Ast——" Heller caught himself. Kaufman smiled forgiveness.

Mary was not the only one in Kaufman's orbit who did not fare well. Franklin Roosevelt's death in April 1945 affected Beatrice Kaufman deeply. She had worked tirelessly in the president's campaign for a fourth term, even while her own health was worsening. On October 6 of that year her heart gave out. Still in her forties, she had a few years earlier embarked on a new extramarital affair with a married man fourteen years younger than she. Beatrice felt a greater love for this last conquest than for previous ones, but George had remained untroubled, knowing that the interdependency he and she enjoyed would not be broken.

Despite their inveterate infidelities, her death left George devastated, and he was certain he would never write again. The man who had always appeared so unemotional now burst into tears at odd moments, and his daughter heard him weep in his sleep.

Four years later, aged sixty, he married Leueen MacGrath, a thirty-five-year-old British actress. Friends were surprised to see how deeply he was in love with her. Nevertheless, on every anniversary of Beatrice's death the seemingly secular playwright lit a *Yahrzeit* candle, used by Jews to commemorate the dead. He stopped only after his daughter, Anne, pointed out that Leueen might be hurt by it.

By 1953 the erstwhile King of Broadway had had a string of flops. Believing that reviewers could no longer be unbiased about a play bearing his name, he suggested to Howard Teichmann, his collaborator on *The Solid Gold Cadillac*, that he not be listed as coauthor. Teichmann wouldn't hear of it, and the play opened to good reviews. To assure himself he had a hit, Kaufman hired a limousine and drove through a snowstorm to gaze at the long lines at the box office.

No longer Ecstasy Man, his union with Leueen became one in name only. After his doctor assured her that George could stand the shock, she told him she was leaving. Now alone in New York, Kaufman assuaged his loneliness by watching television and having

friends over for dinner. When he realized his memory was failing, he gave up all card games. "I'd rather be a poor winner than any kind of loser," he said. He was collaborating on a new comedy with his old friend Marc Connelly shortly before he died on June 2, 1961. His daughter, Anne, and ex-wife, Leueen, were at his side. He was seventy-two.

Franklyn Thorpe remarried and was redivorced by 1947; in the words of his daughter, "His ex took him to the cleaners." In 1954 he hitched up again, this time with the divorcée of a wealthy lawyer. Despite having presided over two thousand Pap smears and half as many births, he never put away a nest egg; the couple lived off her alimony. He died in 1977 at eighty-five.

Marylyn is alive and well at the present writing. She recalls being on the set with her mother when her nanny was away. While

Mary went in and out of marriages, she and her brother were sent to boarding schools. Despite the trauma that she suffered as a child, Marylyn married young and had four children; now she has a total of forty grandchildren and great-grandchildren. "I loved my mother, but was usually scared of her. I never won. She was always right."

Tono, who always liked to fix cars, went on to work for McDonnell Aircraft. He appears to have married twice and had two children.

In 1974, ten years after acting in her last movie, *Hush, Hush, Sweet Charlotte* (1964), Mary entered the Motion Picture Country Home in Woodland Hills, a retirement community then supported by the Motion Picture Relief Fund, with individual cottages and forty-eight acres of walnut and orange groves. Fees were based on ability to pay. Hattie McDaniel, who had won an Oscar for her role in *Gone with the Wind*, lived there. In residence during Mary's stay was Irving Thalberg's widow, Norma Shearer.

By the 1970s Mary had emphysema, heart trouble, and a ruined liver. She needed the on-site medical facilities. She ate her meals in the common dining room, but kept to herself at her own little table. Actors there described a woman who hid her face in a long, hooded housecoat, and discouraged camaraderie. "I visited as often as I could," Marylyn recalled, "but I had children, and she couldn't stand them for more than fifteen minutes."

Regretfully, the arrival of grandchildren hadn't warmed Mary's maternal instincts. Mary often claimed to want just the kind of prosaic life that entailed preparing dinner for a nine-to-five wage earner, but surely at some point she must have accepted that her beauty and talent carried with them a destiny that precluded the ordinary.

After ten years at the Motion Picture Country Home, Mary was spending an increasing amount of time in its well-staffed hospital. That didn't leave much time for writing novels. Her last hadn't been as widely reviewed as the previous two, and she found writing a new one exhausting. She was eighty now, and her ailments were multiplying. On September 25, 1987, in the autumn of Ronald Reagan's presidency, Mary died. The obituary heading in the *New York Times* read, **"Mary Astor, 81, Is Dead; Star of 'Maltese Falcon.'"**

The obit opened by describing her as having had "a delicate beauty, extraordinary grace and a compelling acting style." It pointed out that in her forty-five-year career she had acted in over one hundred movies, and midway down the page described the scandal I had first read about in newspapers under my kitchen linoleum. Little did I imagine half a century ago that Mary Astor would one day take over a good portion of my life. Not quite as large a chunk as, say, Lyndon Johnson has taken out of Robert Caro's life, but quite a bit. Clearly my choice of subject is more difficult to justify than his, but I'll try.

After I read her memoirs and realized she had a gift for writing, I really fell for her. I decided to become her champion, just as—if you'll forgive my presumption—Felix Mendelssohn had become the champion of J. S. Bach and rescued the Baroque composer from relative obscurity. I felt driven to do the same for Mary. Six biographies have been written about Rita Hayworth, ten about Bette Davis, and *sixteen* about Jean Harlow. Mary had nary a one.

Of course, Mary wasn't a reigning Hollywood sex goddess, like Hayworth or Monroe. Her beauty, in all truth, was too aristocratic to be a pinned up in a man's locker. She wasn't even a huge star, and that in itself made me want to shine a light on her. Then too, the fluky way in which I found out about the scandal led me to believe that I was somehow fated to be the keeper of her flame. She was a great actress, and dammit—*I want to see her on a goddam postage stamp!!*

Postscript: In 1952 Mary's diary and its copy were removed by court order from the bank vault where it had sat for sixteen years, and, with a judge standing by, the pages were set aflame and turned to ashes.

The End

Acknowledgments

I've nursed the idea for this book for half a century, but might never have written it if my friend Richard Lingeman hadn't offered to help me with research. Richard, the acclaimed biographer of Theodore Dreiser and Sinclair Lewis, was able to discover arcane material that I would never have found on my own. I owe him big-time.

I couldn't have wished for more enthusiastic editors than Robert Weil and William Menaker. Their close readings and detailed suggestions helped me find the book's final form.

My friend Dan Okrent read early drafts, assured me that I really could write, and urged me to insert more of my own life into the story. Since I know Dan to be right about everything, I chose to believe him.

Prudence Crowther raised frisky questions, shot troubles, and turned many, many phrases. In the chapter where I imagine meeting Mary Astor, she conjured the actress out of a guy from the Bronx. I'm happily indebted to her candor and friendly combat.

About the Author

Edward Sorel is the author of *Unauthorized Portraits* and the illustrator of *First Encounters*, which was written by his late wife, Nancy Caldwell Sorel. His satires and pictorial essays have appeared in *Vanity Fair, Esquire, Atlantic Monthly*, and *The New Yorker*, for which he has done forty-six covers. In 2009 he completed the mural at the Waverly Inn, and two years later the mural for the Monkey Bar, both in New York. His caricatures have been exhibited in the National Portrait Gallery in Washington, DC, and at the Chris Beetles Gallery in London. He is the recipient of the George Polk Award for Satiric Drawing and the *Karikaturpreis der deutschen Anwaltschaft* from the Wilhelm Busch Museum in Hanover, Germany. He lives in Harlem.